Ambulance #11:
Memories of a WWII Veteran

Arthur W. Wolde, Sr.

Published by:
Bluewater Publications
1812 CR 111
Killen, Alabama 35645
www.BluewaterPublications.com

TABLE OF CONTENTS

Art Wolde with the Third Armored Division north of
Bastogne, Belgium, January 1943

PREFACE

This is not only my story; it is also the story of thousands of other ambulance drivers who performed the same duties, encountered the same perils, and shared the same discomforts as I did and am about to describe in this story. It represents their actual lives from the time they left the United States until the war ended. In this case, the combat took place in Europe, but no matter where the battles were fought — North Africa, Sicily, Italy, New Guinea, Guadalcanal, Iwo Jima, Tarawa, Okinawa, or other places in which the fighting took place during World War II — the ambulance corps was always there. Some were continuously at the front; others were relieved and lived through moments of safety when carrying wounded back to the rear. All things considered, they have contributed as equal a share in bringing about the victory as any other branch in the U.S. armed services.

To those who successfully endured the perils and hardships without injury, to those who became prisoners of the enemy, to those who were injured or maimed due to enemy action, and to those who are lying in cemeteries in the fields of France and Belgium, I dedicate this story.

ABOUT THE AUTHOR

The author returned to the Omaha Beach on December 1 and 2, 2005.

He showed his son where he had driven his ambulance ashore. They visited the cemetery that was an apple orchard at that time in 1944. He had parked his ambulance in that area overlooking the English Channel.

They visited Pont du Hoc where the Rangers had scaled the cliffs, then on to Carenton and St. Mere Eglise. Later, they went to Utah Beach, then traveled south to St. Lo and east through Caumont, and back to Bayeau. Returning to Paris via Caen. In Paris, they visited the Eiffel Tower and the Arc de Triomphe.

The author is now 90 years old and in good health.

DEPARTURE

Time: Friday, November 26, 1943
Place: Camp Forrest, Tullahoma, Tennessee

Darkness had settled over Camp Forrest, the flags had been lowered, retreat had been sounded, the mess halls had been emptied out and, except for the occasional whining of the tires of an army vehicle, a stillness was present throughout the camp. This quietness gave little indication that the United States had been at war for almost two years with Germany, Japan, and Italy ever since the sneak attack on Pearl Harbor, Hawaii, on December 7, 1941. So it seemed as if the camp had settled down for another quiet night.

Suddenly, from the headquarters area of the 68th Medical Group (formerly the 68th Medical Regiment) came the sound of a bugle breaking the stillness of the camp and turning it into a scene of activity. But we were expecting it. The day before was Thanksgiving. Some of us had spent the day with our wives, relatives, and friends in Tullahoma and last night we had bid them farewell, knowing we were going to leave, not knowing if or when we would see them again, and wondering what lay ahead for us in the months to come.

We filed out of our barracks and stood in rank in the street. After roll call was made, our first sergeant saluted the company commander and informed him that all were present and accounted for. The 68th Medical Group was ready to leave; the long-expected time had arrived when we would be on our way to take part in the war against Japan and Germany.

As we marched toward the quartermaster depot with our packs on our shoulders and our steel helmets on our head, we didn't have the slightest idea where we were going. There were, of course, three major areas of combat — Europe, Italy, and the Pacific. There was also North Africa, but we didn't think we would be headed in that direction.

We boarded a Pullman troop train at about seven o'clock, and in just a few moments, the train pulled out of the depot. As we pulled out on to the main line, we noticed we were going in a southeasterly direction toward Chattanooga. We then began to guess where our destination would be. Since Camp Shanks, New York was an assembling point for embarkation troops, we assumed that would be our next stop.

Even though I had ridden on a few streamlined trains such as the Tennessean, this was the first time I had ever ridden in a Pullman. I really considered myself as riding in style. Because this was a sleeper, it gave one the impression of riding in class.

We had the opportunity of trying out our berths at about ten p.m. We had spent quite a busy day packing up our equipment and were ready for some sleep. Two men shared the upper berth and two shared the lower berth. I was sharing the lower compartment with my best friend, Herman "Bud" Yehle, when suddenly, about twelve o'clock midnight, we were awakened by a severe jolt. We were sleeping with our heads toward the front of the train, and when it came to a sudden stop, we slid and our heads hit against the front of the berth, and it hurt our necks. The word got around that a coupling had broken and automatically locked the brakes. After about an hour, we started on our way but about thirty minutes later, the same thing happened again.

About this time, our necks were quite sore, and I said to Bud, "It looks like we are going to be casualties before we get to the combat area."

Bud said, "Not me! I am going to do something about this." So, Bud and I decided to sleep the other way so that if it happened a third time, our feet would hit the end of the berth. However, the troop train reached Chattanooga without any further trouble. We were delayed here for several hours while complete repairs were made on the defective couplings. We were told later on that the train had been deliberately tampered with but that it was considered an unsuccessful attempt at sabotage. We left Chattanooga on Saturday morning, November 27, and headed toward the northeast. Now the guessing was over; we felt sure we were moving toward an eastern embarkation area and probably England. Sure enough, we arrived at Camp Shanks, New York after a long and uneventful trip.

We dismounted from the train and carried our duffel bags and packs for what seemed miles (two) to the barracks, which we would occupy during our preparation for overseas. During our stay, we had showdown inspections, medical examinations, and received shots to prevent various diseases we might come in contact with. Our pictures were taken and transferred on medical identification cards that would identify us as medics in case the enemy captured us.

The third night at Camp Shanks, most of us received a twelve-hour pass. Since my hometown was on Long Island and only about one hundred miles away, I decided I would make a trip to see my dad and mom, as I knew it would probably be a long time before I would see them again. Most of the company went to New York, but Bud decided to accept my invitation to

3

come with me, so we slipped in on them secretly. No one in Medford knew I was there but my parents and my brother who was stationed at Camp Shanks. Medford, Long Island was a town in which many German Americans resided and some of the older ones sympathized with Hitler; because of this, I kept this visit a complete secret.

During the two weeks at the camp, I saw my brother Bert occasionally. He was in the signal corps and knew exactly where our next stop would be and even when we would leave this camp, but he could not tell me because of security. However, most of us assumed it was England.

The next big move took place on the night of December 13, when we boarded a train at ten p.m. at the edge of the camp by the side of the Hudson River. The train carried us south toward New York; we crossed the state line into New Jersey and disembarked from the train directly across from Manhattan. Here we boarded a ferry that carried us across to the west side of the big island.

Not far from the ferry, we walked onto a pier alongside a huge ship, which I soon found out was the *Queen Elizabeth*, a British liner, and a magnificent-looking ship during peacetime but now had a coat of battleship gray for war time. A band broke out playing "Roll Out the Barrel" while we walked up the gangplank and entered the side of the *Queen*. A group of us were assigned to a stateroom filled with bunk beds. We slept a while until we heard some motors start, then Lemons, Yehle, and I walked up on the deck. The ship was filled with troops. It was now morning, December 14, and the *Queen Elizabeth* was moving away from the pier. She backed out of the pier with the aid of tugboats and soon was moving forward past the skyscrapers. In front of us was the Statue of Liberty, then, as we passed by the side of the copper lady, I said to Yehle, "I wonder if we will ever see her again."

Soon we were far out in the harbor. Off to the left was the Brooklyn navy yard. Docked at her piers were several battleships, destroyers, and cruisers. My thoughts returned to December 7, 1941. I was returning to Camp Forrest after spending the weekend in Chattanooga, Tennessee, when I heard the disastrous news on a car radio that Pearl Harbor had been attacked by Japanese bombers and that several of our big warships now rested on the floor of the harbor. I later learned in a letter from home that a good friend of mine, Kenneth Wayne of Patchogue, Long Island, had lost his life during the attack and was lying at the bottom of the harbor in the U.S.S. *Maryland*.

As we passed these ships, I thought to myself, *I'm glad they didn't sink all of them*. As the New York harbor faded away, I thought of my parents and my wife, and a sad feeling came over me because I was leaving them behind, but I was comforted with the thought that I was leaving to do my part in defending my country.

Finally, land disappeared from sight and we now had the open sea all around us. It was raining, and the waves were beginning to get high. However, the *Queen Elizabeth* was built to rock forty-five degrees, and being the huge ship that she was, it wasn't too bad. It was very cold, though, so we didn't stay too long on the outer deck. The upper decks were closed in, and there were curtains on the windows that were drawn to at night to keep the lights from being seen on the outside. Each one of us was given a life preserver, and they cautioned us to keep it with us at all times. Most of the time, we kept them on except when we lay down to sleep. We had fire drills and other types of alarms a few times during the trip.

About two days after we left New York, it began to get warm, and we stood on the outer deck without overcoats. I wondered about this, as it was my impression that we were headed for England. We appeared to be moving in a southerly direction, and it was getting warmer. However, the *Queen* was getting out of the shipping lanes and away from most of the German submarine packs that were attacking convoys. The Germans knew that this ship was a troop carrier, so they had been ordered to sink her if the opportunity arose. I learned that there were 17,000 of us aboard this liner, and the Germans knew we were out here, so they were looking for us. We had one advantage, though. The *Queen Elizabeth* was a fast ship and could outrun anything on or below the surface. However, there was the possibility that the subs could locate her position and place themselves ahead of her, so the captain changed course every four minutes.

On the third night out at sea, the ship's engines suddenly stopped and everything was quiet. Rumors immediately began to spread. The first one was that an allied submarine pack was being refueled; however, when we were ordered to switch off as many lights as possible, we knew then that a submarine pack was somewhere ahead. The engines were shut off so they could not pinpoint us, and we were warned not to hit metal with metal. Moments passed, and it was an eerie feeling as we experienced the stillness and the rocking of the ship. Thinking of the deep water we were in, I hung on to my life preserver a little tighter. I could swim just a little and never did learn how to float; thus, the little swimming I could do wouldn't keep me up very long, so my life preserver was a friend to me.

Also, I could imagine about a hundred sharks swimming around the ship. I remembered the hurricane of August 1938 when a new inlet broke through Fire Island near Mastic, Long Island, and three hammerhead sharks entered into the Great South Bay. They were finally caught and their pictures were shown in the local papers. I could envision myself being dragged down into the water by a huge shark. It's surprising, really, what thoughts will come into one's mind at a time like this.

After what seemed like hours, the motors started again, and the ship moved on. Tension eased and we relaxed once more. The rest of the trip was uneventful. It took eight days to cross the Atlantic Ocean because we had gone eight hundred miles out of the regular course. Normally, it took the *Queen Elizabeth* four days to travel from England to New York.

ENGLAND

The blackout curtains were still closed on the promenade deck of the *Queen* when we heard the news that the ship was moving slowly into the harbor of the Firth of Clyde in Scotland on the morning of December 22. At 7:20 a.m., they let us out on the outside deck for a short time, and we had our first glimpse of Great Britain. It looked strange to us, quite different from the land we had left behind.

We looked forward to beginning our travel from the port to the place where we would stay during the time we would be in England, but it wasn't until the next day that we left the ship and boarded a train. It was going to be a long trip, so they handed out several boxes to us that had a shape like a box of crackerjacks. It was K rations, which consisted of a package of biscuits, a can of meat, a pack of four cigarettes, and a bar of chocolate or candy.

We started on our way south, and as we passed through towns, the children were standing by the railroad tracks yelling for candy and gum. Since we had just come from the States, we were well supplied with these things, so we threw something out occasionally to them. This was probably a well-traveled troop-train route, and when the children heard a train coming, they would run to the tracks and wait.

The train was an odd-looking one, but it was very fast. I had traveled on the express trains between New York and Washington at speeds of eighty and ninety miles an hour, but on this train, it seemed as if I were traveling faster than I had ever traveled before.

The next morning, we rolled into Goring, about thirty miles west of London and twenty miles east of Oxford. They carried us in trucks to a British army camp, which was to be our new home for a while. We were restricted to the camp area for seven days. On Christmas day, at the edge of the camp area, we wished the children who came around a Merry Christmas. Candy and chocolate were something rare to them, so it was a real treat when we passed it out.

Our company was invited to a New Year's Eve dance, and after being restricted to the area, we welcomed the opportunity to look at and get acquainted with the people of England. They loaded us up in trucks and carried us to a church in Reading, about seven miles from the camp. A few hours here helped to take the gloom away, as we were beginning to feel sorry for ourselves. Midnight came and the year 1944 came into existence.

The first few days we were in England, it was very quiet. The Germans must have been observing the holidays also, as there were no air raids. But not long after the first of January and at night, we heard the sirens going off. As we looked toward London, we could see the ack-ack explode and tracer bullets streaming through the sky. Even though the city was thirty miles away, we had an excellent view from our camp area.

Early one morning, those of us in the ambulance platoon were loaded up on trucks and carried to Bristol, England. Here, in a large field, thousands of vehicles were dispersed. They were well spread out so that in the event of an air attack, only a few would be destroyed by one bomb. We drove to an area where there were ten ambulances, numbered from 7 to 16. They told each one of us to take an ambulance. Grant Trader took #7; Chaffin, #8; Kosty, #9; and Jones, #10; I took #11; Yehle, #12; Volz, #13; Leuck, #14; Ables, #15; and Wilmes, #16. We climbed into the ambulances, drove out of the field, and headed back toward our camp. Immediately out on the road, we had to get used to something that we were unfamiliar with — driving on the left side of the road. That's the way the British do it, and being in their country, we had to do likewise. It seemed odd at first, but we soon got accustomed to it.

The air raids over London were almost nightly. During the month of February, the Germans stepped up their attacks, especially on London. One night, one of the German planes appeared to be in trouble and it flew almost directly over the camp. Not too far from us — between Reading and Goring — the pilot dropped his bombs. The plane was probably hit before he made his bombing run, and he ditched his bombs here hoping he could make it back to occupied France or Germany.

On Saturday, February 23, Yehle and I drew a pass to London and that night, we experienced a large air raid on the city. First the air-raid sirens sounded, warning the residents that the enemy was coming over the channel. Then, off to the east, Yehle and I saw ack-ack bursting and tracers shooting up into the sky. We looked up to where the searchlights were pinpointed together. As we began to hear the roar of the planes, we saw them outlined in the beams of searchlights. By this time, all of the civilians were off the streets and in the air-raid shelters, houses, and cellars.

Being soldiers, we were not allowed to go into the air-raid shelters and take up a space where a civilian could stay, so we had to find the best shelter we could. We got under a covered porch to protect us from falling flak. Almost immediately, it began to fall upon the street where we had been a few seconds before. It sounded like golf-ball-size hailstones hitting the streets. By this time, the planes were almost directly overhead, and we both began to get a tense feeling, hoping they wouldn't unload any bombs on this area.

Bombs were exploding in different parts of the city, and fire engines were rushing to the burning areas. Rescue squads were also dispatched in case any civilians were trapped in the wreckage. We saw the planes receive direct hits, explode, and begin diving to the ground.

The searchlights began to concentrate on something floating down. The British had many barrage balloons over the city. At first, we thought one of these had been punctured. As it came closer, we saw that it was a parachute. In the London papers the next day, we read they had captured a young German airman who was seventeen years old. Sunday morning there was another alert, but it was only an enemy reconnaissance plane taking pictures of the damage that was done the night before. For the remainder of the month, we viewed several more serious raids on London from our camp near Goring.

March came and we went through training periods similar to the training we had back in the States. We did first-echelon maintenance on our ambulances occasionally. In the evenings, we took walks to visit the small villages around the camp and chat with the civilians. The days were beginning to get longer, and it was still daylight even after we arrived back at the camp from the walks. I bought a bicycle and was in style with the rest of the English, as a bicycle was all that most of them could afford. Yehle bought one as well and on Sundays, we took longer rides.

We received a month's training on the care and operation of a rifle. The purpose of this was for protection in case of attack by guerilla bands. If this occurred, we would be armed with rifles to protect ourselves. At the end of the month, they took us out to a firing range to check our shooting skill. I scored 92% — 69 out of 75, nine fives (bull's-eyes) and six fours. This was not bad for the first time I had ever fired a rifle in my life. During the training, we used 03 Springfields, but on the firing range, we used M-1s.

April came and Lemons (my assistant driver) and I were sent on detached service with the 65th Armored Field Artillery Battalion at Coventry, about seventy-five miles north of London. Coventry was one of the cities hit by the Luftwaffe (German Air Force), so we experienced a little more of what the British people had been going through. We also underwent several air raids on this city while we worked there, but with the British and American air artillery combined, the planes didn't tarry too long. In fact, some of them never got back to Germany, as they were shot down. Almost every day in April, there were one thousand plane raids over Germany, and as the American bombers left in the morning, they would fly over Coventry. Sometimes, when they came back in the afternoon, it was not too pleasant a sight. Sometimes there would be a vacant spot in a squadron where a B-17 Flying Fortress bomber had been when they left in the morning. Some of the planes would have parts of the wings shot off; others would have big holes in the fuselage. Some of them would come back with only two or three engines operating; others would trail behind and come in on a wing and a prayer.

Although our medical group had not yet experienced combat, it made us realize that much more that we were at war. At night, it was the Royal Air Force's (RAF) turn. They went out and made huge raids on the German cities. The casualties were heavy, but the Germans were getting a taste of what they were handing out. No doubt, the RAF suffered losses as well, but we didn't see them come back as we were sleeping when they returned.

Our work was to carry sick GIs to the general hospitals in Oxford. One morning, on the way back to Coventry, part of the rubber on the right rear tire of #11 peeled off (about eighteen inches of it). I stopped immediately, and Lemons and I changed tires. When we got to Coventry, I carried the tire to a maintenance outfit and put in a requisition for a new one. Although we checked our ambulances regularly, I thought it might have been my fault. However, the maintenance men told me this was a synthetic rubber tire and that part of the rubber had not adhered properly to the rest of the tire.

We didn't have too many trips to Oxford and life became kind of dull hanging around not doing much. When the letter writing to the home folks was finished, we would stroll around the nearby area and get a fish covered with potato chips. These were wrapped in a newspaper sheet and the English called them "fish and chips." After several weeks, we returned to our own medical group.

Our sergeants took us out to the motor pool one morning and gave each of us a large can of asbestos waterproofing compound. They showed us how to cover our spark plugs, wires, all electrical parts, and all parts necessary to prevent water damage to the vehicle — also around the doors of the ambulance. When we had each vehicle completely waterproofed, we had to crawl in through the door windows. Then we drove our ambulances a short distance to what looked like a lake. Actually, it was nothing more than a man-made hole four and a half feet deep, long enough and wide enough for an ambulance to be driven around in. The sergeants told us each vehicle with the waterproofing was capable of running around in the water for about fifteen minutes. What we wondered about was how we would get them from the ship into the salt water. We found that out in just about two months.

May came and the days began to get longer. Since we were much farther north in England than we had been in our own country, it was unusual for us to see the sun set so late in the evening and daylight at ten p.m. as the days passed, the sun set even later than ten p.m.

The month of May was quite a busy one for us. Several mornings, our sergeants took us to an airfield where we received training on loading wounded onto C-47 air transport planes. We would carry the wounded on litters from our ambulances and strap the litters in place on the transport. After several hours of training, we were given a ride on one of the transports. This was my first ride on a plane. I had signed up for the air corps as my choice of service, but they put me in the medics instead. After this ride, however, I wasn't too disappointed anymore. It was a rough ride and when the plane hit several air pockets, most of us got sick. I don't think I have to explain any further, but our steel helmets served many a purpose beside protection for our heads.

Several days after our trip to the airfield, some of the other ambulance outfits were receiving training on the transports. It was in the morning and I was pulling my last two hours on guard duty at the camp. As I walked my post, I approached a flagpole with our American flag waving proudly in the breeze. At that moment, a C-47 swooped down over camp. Unfortunately, the pilot came down a little too low. As he began his upward swing, the tail section hit the flagpole with such force that the flagpole ripped into one of the barracks and smashed into an army cot. Fortunately, no one was in the barracks. The right tail section of the plane was sheared off and when it fell, it missed me by inches. I called for the sergeant of the guard and soon the area as filled with officers and men. I expected the plane to crash, but it flew on as if nothing had happened. I heard later that it reached the airfield safely.

I was called to the company headquarters one morning and handed a cablegram that read, "BABY DIED; WIFE DOING FINE." My newborn daughter, Patricia Ann, died two days after birth. One of our chaplains, Captain McBarron, drove me to Reading and I sent a cablegram to my wife that read, "TOGETHER WE SHARE IN SORROW."

Toward the end of the month, everyone was getting invasion minded. It seemed as if a smash into France might be near. We had been warned several times on security and on May 25, 1944, our company had a meeting in which we were once more cautioned. The Germans were predicting an invasion on various days according to a British newspaper, *The London Times*, but England and the United States were keeping silent. We were suspecting that something was about to happen, as the Germans were claiming that an enormous armada of ships was massing at the southern ports of England. We sold our bicycles.

The last week the company was placed on restriction and confined to the camp area. Rumors spread like wildfire throughout the camp. This was one reason we were placed on restriction so that nothing would leak out to the civilians. Among them were enemy agents and one slip could be disastrous to the whole plan. The Germans did not know where the invasion point would be. Of course, we didn't know either but we couldn't afford leaks of any sort. Finally, one morning we loaded up our ambulances with barracks bags and moved out. We drove south to a wooded area outside of Portsmouth, England, where we set up our pup tents and bivouacked for a few days. We welcomed the change, as time began to grow monotonous at the camp. What we didn't know was that during the next sixteen months, time would be occupied so that we wouldn't have a moment to be bored again. Just before we left this bivouac area, we received a letter from General Eisenhower notifying us that we were about to embark upon a great crusade and that the eyes of the world would be upon us. In spite of knowing that danger awaited us, we couldn't help having a feeling of pride.

SUPREME HEADQUARTERS

ALLIED EXPENDITONARY FORCES

Soldiers, Sailors, and Airmen of the Allied Expeditionary Force!

You are about to embark upon the Great Crusade, toward which we have striven these many months. The eyes of the world are upon you. The hopes and prayers of liberty-loving people everywhere march with you. In company with our brave Allies and brothers-in-arms on other Fronts, you will bring about the destruction of the German war machine, the elimination of Nazi tyranny over the oppressed peoples of Europe, and security for ourselves in a free world.

Your task will not be an easy one. Your enemy is well trained, well equipped, and battle-hardened. He will fight savagely.

But this is the year 1944! Much has happened since the Nazi triumphs of 1940-41. The United Nations have inflicted upon the Germans great defeats, in open battle, man-to-man. Our air offensive has seriously reduced their strength in the air and their capacity to wage war on the ground. Our Home Fronts have given us an overwhelming superiority in weapons and munitions of war, and placed at our disposal great reserves of trained fighting men. The tide has turned! The free men of the world are marching together to Victory!

I have full confidence in your courage, devotion to duty, and skill in battle. We will accept nothing less than full Victory!

Good Luck! And let us all beseech the blessing of Almighty God upon this great and noble undertaking.

Dwight D. Eisenhower

About May 30, we loaded our ambulances up again with bags and personal equipment and drove to a marshaling area at Portsmouth, England. We drove our ambulances on to a pier and waterproofed them again, then boarded a liberty ship, the S.S. *James Woodworth*, with the rest of the company. That night, we were under a bombing raid. The Germans were trying to break up the armada or inflict as much damage as possible. Some of the bombs dropped close to the ships, but none of them were hit. The next morning, we stood on the deck, watching our ambulances be lifted from the dock and lowered into the hold of the ship. Night came and they were still loading our ship with equipment and vehicles. We stayed by the side of the pier until noon of the next day; then we sailed out and anchored in the harbor. To the north, to the south, and to the east and west were what seemed like countless numbers of liberty ships and invasion craft. Some of the ships had doors on the front which when lowered, became ramps and I thought at this moment that our vehicles would be transferred over to one of them, but we found out differently later on.

The next morning, June 3, we began to move slowly again. We were probably being placed into position as part of this great invasion fleet. Thousands of boats of all kinds were in front of us and behind us, some by the sides of us, all of us being protected by corvettes. These fast little British warships were equipped with antiaircraft guns and depth charges to ward off the enemy planes and submarines.

We were approximately one hundred miles from the coast of France and knew that in a short time the invasion would begin. Where it would take place we still did not know, but the Germans had predicted the location would be Le Havre, Cherbourg, or the Cherbourg peninsula. Numerous places were being bombed by planes and shelled by warships in an effort to confuse the Germans.

As we moved out of the harbor of the Firth of Forth and toward the England Channel, we looked over to the left. In the distance, we noticed some white cliffs. These resembled the white cliffs of Dover, of which I had seen pictures. It was a magnificent sight to see these huge white walls towering upward. Finally, they disappeared from sight and we were out in the channel.

The weather began to get rough; there were frequent rainsqualls and the waves began to get choppy. There was a feeling of tenseness as we moved on toward the French coast. For most of us, this was our first invasion and we had no idea what an invasion would be like. Several times we stopped but whether we stopped or moved on, we were prime targets for U-boats. However, we felt a certain amount of security with the corvettes by the side of us to chase away the submarines.

On and on we sailed. A southeasterly course seemed to be our direction of travel. The entire day of June 5 passed without an incident. We would have to come back to our bunks occasionally, as sometimes the rain would come down pretty heavily. There was no sight of land in front us yet and no indication of what lay ahead. The excitement of the immediate future interrupted our sleeping pattern, so we would sleep when we got tired. This meant some of us might be standing on the deck during the dark hours of the morning. Such was the case for Yehle and me sometime after midnight and on the morning of June 6. Suddenly, from behind us came the roar of an enormous armada of planes. As they passed overhead, we could see the silhouettes of C-47s against the sky. Each plane was towing a glider and each glider was filled with a number of troops. An entire airborne division was on its way and would soon be landing in France. As the gliders would disconnect from the C-47s, they would glide to a landing. The troops would get out and start to attack the Germans wherever they could. They kept as many Germans occupied as possible, thus easing the task for the forces that would land on the beach.

INVASION BY THE FIRST ARMY, U.S.A.

Since thirty minutes had elapsed after the C-47s had passed over, I assume it would be safe to say that the invasion of France had begun. Now, from the bow of the ship, we could see bright flashes and hear rumblings like thunder. It seemed as if it were a thunder and lightning storm ahead, but it was actually shells being fired on the French coast from U.S. and British warships. Later as we moved closer, red glows began to rise over the horizon, and we figured between ourselves that either ships were hit or enemy coastal installations were being shelled and were on fire. What we didn't know was that the landing forces were smashing ashore, the LSTs had beached, and men and tanks were pushing inland to join up with the paratroopers we had seen in the gliders several hours before.

We anchored a few miles off the coast of Normandy at an area between the cities if Isigny and Caen. From this point, we could see a large fire ahead; it was at the shoreline. Columns of smoke were also rising from places inland. It was several hours into the daylight now, and we could plainly see the LSTs on the edge of the beach. One of them was burning. Shells were landing in the water about a mile ahead of us. Our ship was out of reach of the enemy artillery, but there were other vessels ahead of us, including some of our battleships, which were close enough for directs.

Suddenly, trace bullets began to shoot up into the sky from all directions. The antiaircraft guns on the front of our ship also blasted away. We watched where the bullets narrowed together and saw an enemy plane diving downward. It was a bomber. A few seconds later, not far from us, a liberty ship was hit. It started to blaze, and smoke started to pour from it. The bomber sped away, but not until it had received extensive damage from antiaircraft fire. Other ships began to close in on the burning vessel to remove casualties and pick up men as they evacuated the ship. We heard later that it split in two and sank.

It was now mid morning, and we could see numerous columns of smoke rising from the higher ground behind the beach, probably coming from shelled enemy fortifications or civilian homes and buildings. According to reports coming in, Hitler was boasting that he was going to throw us off the beachhead and back into the sea as he had the British at Dunkirk, but by this time, our invasion forces had pushed inland, joined up with the airborne troops, and were well established. This beachhead was one of the two landings; another beachhead was made just west of Isigny at the south end and east side of the Cotentin peninsula. The idea of this landing was to smash across the peninsula and cut off the city of Cherbourg on the north end where quite a few German troops were stationed.

Sometime during the morning, a call was made to our ship for medical help. Our vessel started to move toward the shore, and we maneuvered in close to the side of a high cliff that we used as a shelter. A small boat pulled alongside us, and the litter bearer and station platoons of our company went over the side of the ship and climbed down on rope ladders to the smaller vessel. They were taken ashore. As yet, it was impossible for our ambulances to be landed, as the water was still rough. Only those ambulances that were on the LSTs were ashore.

While we at the beach, we saw wreckage and equipment scattered everywhere. We saw burned-out American tanks, wrecked jeeps, boats other than the LSTs we saw grounded on the beach turned upside down — including the one we saw burning quite a few hours before. Our men were picking up bodies of Americans, who were now almost covered by sand carried in by the rough waves. These men had been cut down by machine-gun fire as they left the LSTs and stormed ashore.

By this time, the enemy artillery guns had been destroyed or pushed back to where they were no longer a threat to the ships or the shoreline. Our ship pulled out and we anchored about a half-mile from shore. About one-half mile behind us was the U.S.S. *Texas* and the U.S.S. *Nevada*. These two battleships were doing a great job in assisting the ground troops, as a problem existed in the area. Hedgerows divided most of the civilian property. At the border of each civilian's plot of land was a hedgerow to the north, to the south, to the east, and to the west. Looking down from above, they looked like a bunch of rectangles and squares just as far as you could see. They extended toward the south for at least twenty miles, almost as far south as the city of St. Lo. The German had an effective gun hidden in those hedgerows — a modern 88 mm antiaircraft gun that they found out could be successfully useful against our armored tanks. Almost every hedgerow had an 88 hidden in it somewhere, so it was slow going for our tanks and troops. When our ground forces spotted one, they would radio back its position to the battleships, which, in turn, would zero in on it and knock it out. So it was a one hedgerow to another hedgerow affair for a while, becoming more difficult when our forces pushed south and out of range of the big guns on the ships.

For several days, our ears were exposed to the deafening roar of the guns on the battleships as they fired over our heads. We soon got used to it and stood on the deck watching as the big ones fired away. This lasted for a couple of days until their range became ineffective.

We stayed on the boat for six days. During this time, the weather began to clear up, the channel calmed down, and the water around us became like a sea of glass. When it cleared and the sun appeared in a cloudless sky, I beheld a magnificent sight. The water between our ship and the shoreline had a beautiful blue tint. As I leaned against the rail of the ship, admiring this magnificent scene of the pretty blue water and the beach, I thought to myself, *What a pity for one of God's creations to be marred up like this, not because we had chosen this area for the invasion but because of the ruthless dictatorship of one man who was bent on world domination.* However, in spite of the scarred shoreline, it was still a splendid sight to behold. Surely, the French people must have been proud of this wonderful beach.

It was now June 12 and in the afternoon, our ambulances were lifted out of the hold by a huge crane and lowered onto a box pontoon barge. In front of the barge was a ramp from which we would drive off into the water. Now we understood how we were going to get our vehicles onto the land in front us as well as the purpose of the waterproofing. There was a low tide, but it was still too deep for our ambulances from where we were. Therefore, we had to wait until the next morning so the barge could get closer to the beach, close enough for us to drive into water that would be about four and one-half feet deep. We were

23

anxious to get off the ship and onto land, but this meant we would have to spend another night on the water.

During the dark hours of the morning of June 13, we were awakened by the sound of antiaircraft fire from the shore and the ships. Thousands of 90 mm, 40 mm, 37 mm guns, and .50 caliber machine guns were pointed upward at an enemy plane that was snooping around. Lt. Gen. Omar Bradley's air defense officer disclosed that all these guns constituted the greatest concentration of antiaircraft fire in military history. The German plane kept up very high and flew away quickly. The guns quieted down, and we dozed off again, but not for very long, as the sergeants woke us up. We climbed over the side of the ship and descended on a chain ladder to the barge; then we crawled into the driver's side of our ambulances. We catnapped again for a while until the barge started to move and woke us up.

We moved in, and when we were about a tenth of a mile from the beach, the barge stopped. Ambulance #11 was first in line and ready to descend off the ramp. We got the order to shove off, and as I looked at the ramp, I thought to myself, *Now the test is about to begin to see what kind of waterproofing job Lemons and I have done.* Down off the ramp we went, and water came over the hood of #11. Suddenly, to our dismay, the motor of #11 stalled about five feet from the ramp.

"Oh, man," I said to Lemons, "did we goof?"

All kinds of thoughts ran through my mind. Was that water over my head? After all, I wasn't too good a swimmer. We had been trained to drive through four and a half feet or five feet of salt water, but when the engine stalled, it looked like six feet or more.

But, almost immediately, we discovered the trouble. From the carburetor on top of the motor stretched a rubber hose three inches wide that extended into the inside of the ambulance through the window opening on the right side of #11. The hose drew air into the carburetor from the inside of the ambulance. The window was lowered just enough to let the hose through. The inside of #11 behind our seats was loaded with barracks bags and laundry bags belonging to the men of the company. One of the laundry bags was drawn into the hose opening, cutting off the air to the carburetor.

Lemons pulled it out of the hose and threw it well out of the way. I did the natural thing that everyone does when a motor stalls, I stepped on the starter button and to my relief, the motor started. I was surprised when it started. Later on, when I had time to think it over, I realized that was exactly what it should have done since the engine was completely waterproofed. Still, I figured that I had accomplished something that I don't believe anyone else had done — I had started a stalled motor in four and a half feet of water.

Comforted with that experience behind me, I drove through the water and up onto the beach. We drove up a hill to high ground and made our camp in an apple orchard where we immediately began to remove the waterproofing compound from the motors of our ambulances. Not a drop of water got into #11, proving that Lemons and I had done a good job of waterproofing.

Off to the side of the apple orchard, a cemetery was being dug and bodies of GIs were already being placed into four-by-six-by-six-feet holes. French men and women from the area were kneeling and praying for the dead Americans.

Up until this time, we had not known where we were, but we found out that the beachhead that we landed on was called the Omaha Beachhead, which was sixty miles southeast of the city of Cherbourg. About a mile in front of us was the village of Saint-Laurent-sur-Mer. Also in front of us were the hedgerows I previously mentioned.

While we were in the orchard, we witnessed several air raids. When things got "hot," we would crawl under our ambulances for protection against falling shrapnel. We dug foxholes, and they were fairly good shelter against bombs but ineffective against our own shrapnel, which was falling around the beach like whistling rain. As we lay under the ambulances, we would hear it bounce off the top of our vehicles with a loud noise like hail, only much louder. The shrapnel was more dangerous than bombs, because the enemy planes were staying clear of the antiaircraft fire, and the danger of a bomb being dropped was very slight.

We were on "standby," and there wasn't much for us to do, so we took short walks around the area above the beach. There was an unpleasant stench around that we had to get accustomed to; it was the smell of the dead. Not only humans but also animals suffered the results of war. We passed dead dogs, cats, horses, and cows all lying on the roadside. We were warned to stay on well-traveled roads and to keep out of fields and hedgerows because of booby traps, mines, and explosives that might not have been discovered. On one of these walks, we came upon the bodies of three dead Germans whom they had not yet had time to bury. One of these had on an American sergeant's uniform. He must have killed a sergeant and put his uniform on so he could get close to other GIs in order to kill

26

them. He must have been discovered, and they killed him right on the spot.

Other times we passed unexploded shells that were boxed off and encircled with white tape. We also saw some of the German 88s in the hedgerows. We didn't get close to them. We stayed on the roads, but we could see the gun barrels sticking out of the hedges. Some were disabled and others were in perfect condition.

During one walk, we came in sight of Saint-Laurent-sur-Mer. In the middle of the town was a church that had a huge hole in the tower near the bell. We were told that a French girl about eighteen, who had a German-soldier boyfriend, was sniping at Americans. They brought up an American tank that fired at the church, putting the hole in the tower. Later on, they found pieces of her.

Forty-fifth Evacuation Hospital in operation at LaCambe, France

Our bivouac area at evacuation hospital LaCambe, France

The front line was now fifteen miles inland, and it was on June 26 that our entire company got together again. We moved three or four miles inland and were attached to the 24th Evacuation Hospital at Lacambe. This was near several American fighter plane fields and about eleven miles from the front line, on a main highway from Caen to Cherbourg. The same afternoon, we heard the roar of planes. As we looked up into the sky, we witnessed an air battle in progress. Several German fighters had come around and within five minutes, fifty of our Thunderbolts and Mustangs had taken to the air, intercepted the enemy, and were engaged in an air battle. As we watched, we saw a column of smoke trail behind one of the German fighters, and down it went.

We had an opportunity to visit the fighter strips, look over the planes, and talk to the pilots. Most of pilots had small swastikas painted on the sides of their planes, the number according to how many German fighters each had shot down.

As I stood at a crossroad one afternoon, an event took place that I will always remember. As we happened to look down the road toward the fighter fields, a jeep came along, and on the helmet of one of the occupants was painted four stars. We immediately snapped to attention, saluted, then had the privilege of meeting General Eisenhower in person. General "Ike" smiled, waved, and said, "Hi, fellers," as the jeep rounded the corner and headed toward Isigny and Cherbourg.

Here with the 24th Evacuation Hospital our work began. We began to transport wounded to the airfields at the beach, especially to one near the apple orchard where we had temporarily bivouacked for a few days after we had left the ship.

June 2, 1944, was the day that our forces captured the city of Cherbourg. Three days later, our ambulances and hundreds of others were called upon to carry wounded Germans from hospitals in Cherbourg to the Utah beachhead, which was near Isigny from where they were to be transported in hospital ships to British hospitals or POW camps.

We rendezvoused at the apple orchard, and at 4:30 in the morning, we started on our way toward Cherbourg. We passed through Isingy. There were civilians in this city, but it would be hard to say where they were living because the city was completely destroyed. On toward Carentan we traveled, not realizing we would be experiencing what you might call our firs actual baptism of fire. At this city, the front was only one-half mile to the southwest and well within range of enemy artillery fire. The Germans were dropping shells into the city, concentrating on the road we were traveling and trying to knock out a bridge we had to cross. We didn't waste any time getting through Carentan.

Two more towns — St. Mere Eglise and Valognes — were also destroyed. Leaving these behind, we began to pass by fields in which there were wrecked gliders, the ones that flew over us when we were still in the channel. We finally came into the city of Cherbourg and noticed that his city was not quite as damaged as some of the other cities or towns we had passed through. We arrived at the hospital, from which we had to evacuate, at nine a.m. and ate our breakfast of K rations. We were getting kind of sick of them because we had to use them quite often as we were frequently away from our company or the evacuation hospital. But we still considered ourselves fortunate because many of the civilians had nothing to eat.

"Littleman" (Lemons) and I picked up our first load of Germans and transported them to the Utah beachhead. As we passed through the shelling at Carentan, we thought, *Well, if they kill us, they will be killing some of their own also.* Leaving the German prisoners at the beachhead, we returned to Cherbourg and found out that we were relieved. On the way back to Lacambe, we noticed that the shelling had ceased in Carentan, and we completed the rest of the trip without incident.

On July 9, our company moved one-half mile to become temporarily attached to the 45th Evacuation Hospital in the same town. We were still evacuating to the airstrips at the beach, but at times, we had to go to some of the damaged towns to pick up wounded civilians and carry them to French civilian hospitals. With all of the destruction and death around

German Prisoner

Some of Company C enlisted men at the Twenty-
fourth Evacuation Hospital Area at La Cambe, July
1944

us, it wasn't hard for us to realize that we were engaged in a large-scale war. I looked at the parts of building that were still standing, then I thought of home and how fortunate we and everyone else in American were.

While at the 45th Evacuation Hospital, we experienced quite a few air raids at night, but before any damage was done, the enemy planes were either run off or shot down. Quite a few of them were hit by antiaircraft fire an exploded into a ball of fire that fell from the sky like a comet.

After returning from the beach one evening, we stopped at an American cemetery. Here we took pictures of the bodies of Americans lying in graves not yet covered. They were wrapped in white cloth and were being temporarily kept this way until coffins were available. As we stood there, we heard the sputtering of engines in the sky. Glancing up, we saw a B-24 Liberator in trouble. It was circling around not far from us, and we began to wonder what was going to happen. We didn't have to wonder too long before suddenly, in the sky there were seven parachutes. Immediately, the Liberator turned into a downward dive; it hit the ground, and we saw a column of smoke shoot upward into the air. A few seconds later, we heard the sound of the crash. We returned to the hospital, parked #11, and walked to the scene of the wreckage, which was not far from the hospital. Fortunately, it crashed in an open field. One of the motors was buried about six feet into the ground. The rest of the plane was lying all over the field. We heard later that everyone had gotten out of the plane safely.

On July 9, Yehle and I were informed that we had been appointed to perform a mission. Sixteen nurses, who were among the personnel at the German hospitals in Cherbourg, were given the choice of staying on the Allied side and caring for the German wounded or returning to the German side. They chose to go back to Germany. Two other ambulances in our outfit had already returned eight of them. Now we had been selected to carry the other eight over into the German lines and turn them over to the Germans. We covered our rear windows and hung blankets from the top of the ambulance behind the driver's seat so that they couldn't look out and report anything to the Nazis. We left the 45th Evacuation Hospital and proceed to Caumont, a city south of Lacambe.

Railroad depot and tracks destroyed at Travierres, south of LaCambe, July 1944

At Caumont, five miles from the front lines, we had to wait until a cease-fire and a one-hour truce could be made with the Germans. When the time came for the truce, the firing stopped, and we began to move forward through the city of Caumont. This city was also a mass of rubble, and at time, we had to drive up over piles of rubble six feet high, consisting of debris from wrecked buildings. We drove cautiously and followed other tracks because this city had not yet been checked for mines. The moments here were tense, and we were hoping we would not strike a mine. We came to a road block where, stretched across the road, was a line of mines. Captain Quentin Roosevelt, a nephew of the late President "Teddy" Roosevelt, was standing by and when he kicked the mines to the side of the road, our hearts jumped about five inches. Although we had expected them to explode, only a heavy vehicle would have set them off. Having been warned about mines and booby traps, we eyed them cautiously.

Captain Roosevelt jumped onto the running board of #11 and told me to move forward. Yehle followed in #12 and we rounded a turn in the road, driving over the ruins of another building. Just as we passed this wreckage, two Germans jumped on the right running board and smiled. It seemed strange. Just a short time ago, two sides fighting one another; now Germans smiling at us, and a short time later, shooting at each other again.

As we moved forward, we saw standing in the road in front us several German officers and an American officer, who was an interpreter. We stopped the ambulance. Captain Roosevelt walked up to them, and they saluted one another. Yehle and I let the nurses out, and while the interpreter talked, we stood with the German soldiers and swapped cigarettes with them. We didn't try to speak because we knew we couldn't understand each other. They helped us to turn around because they knew where their mines were and where it was safe.

We then returned to the north side of Caumont and had the privilege of meeting Ernest Hemingway, a famous news correspondent and column writer. He asked us questions, and we told him about the events that took place during the truce. Several days later, the news of this event was published in the main newspapers all over the United States and probably all over the world. While we were talking to Mr. Hemingway, the guns opened up, and war broke loose again.

On July 21, we (the 45th Medical Collecting Company) moved to Airel, pulled into a field next to the 24th Evacuation Hospital, and began to unload our equipment. Our men were setting up their pup tents when one of our staff sergeants, Sergeant Norton, received a gunshot wound. The bullet struck him in the thigh slightly above the knee as he was kneeling in the back of his personal equipment. Since we were about seven miles from the front lines, we assumed it was a sniper's bullet, and we felt uneasy for a few days. It was reported, however, and a search was made for all the civilian guns in the homes surrounding the area. This was the first time we had been fired on by a sniper, and he was the first casualty in the company.

During this week, we witnessed an aerial bombardment of St. Lo. The First Army had worked their way out of the hedgerows, but the Nazis were making a stubborn stand at this city. Early one morning, several smoke bombs were shot up into the air by ground troops so that the bombers would know their positions and could drop their bombs ahead of the smoke and on the Germans. First came a mass of P-47 Thunderbolt dive-bombers with small bombs under their carriages. They dive bombed the German side so as to drive the Germans into

Outskirts of St. Lo, France

their trenches, but before the heavy bombers (the B-17s) arrived over the marked area, a very unfortunate thing happened. The smoke drifted faster than they had estimated it would and had drifted back toward our lines. Some of the bombs dropped a little short of their targets. Lieutenant General McNair was watching from an area overlooking St. Lo when he was struck and killed by bomb fragments. After the B-17s, a mass of B-25 light bombers came over and dropped their bombs. Then, the First Army attacked the city, the Germans fled, and St. Lo was in our hands. One of these light bombers developed some kind of trouble, however, before it arrived at the bombing area and dropped its bombs one-tenth of a mile from the 24th Evacuation Hospital, almost on top of us. A number of men from another

Village in St. Lo area completely destroyed, July 1944

military unit were injured, and we were immediately summoned to the area to carry them to the hospital. Also, at the time the bombing occurred, one of our staff sergeants, Sergeant Pierce, was returning to the company from a trip. Just as he came up on the area, the bomb exploded, and a fragment came through the vehicle and embedded itself behind the driver's seat narrowly missing him by a fraction of an inch.

The solider that Lemons and I picked up had a huge hole in his chest. As I drove to the hospital, a medic held bandages on the wound and used pressure to slow down the hemorrhaging. He died at the hospital from loss of blood before anything could be done for him. This was the first time that I had seen one of our men dying, and it made all of us realize more and more that we were getting into the thick of the battle. Also, that very same day, we heard that an attempt had been made on Hitler's life but that it was unsuccessful and some of his top-ranking officers had been executed.

We experienced another air raid one night while we were at Airel, and three planes were shot down. One exploded in the air, turning into an orange ball of flame as it began its dive to the ground. It wasn't too far from the hospital, so we walked to the wreckage. While I was there, I met a hometown friend of mine, Bill Hahn, Jr., also from Medford, New York. He was with an outfit about three miles from our bivouac area. Seeing him was a morale boost for each of us because neither of us had, until now, met any one of our friends from home. Even though we had friends in our outfits, it helped us that much more to feel that we were not alone.

On July 28, our company moved to Marigny, which was east of St. Lo and about seventy miles south of the beachhead. The First and Third Armies were racing down the coast through a strip about thirty miles wide in an attempt to cut off the Brittany peninsula. We spent several days here. One morning we noticed a B-17 circling around and on fire. Shortly afterward, it crashed not too far from us, and we ran to the field where it crashed. When we arrived, we saw the wreckage strewn out on the ground for about one-fourth of a mile. We didn't hear whether there were any casualties or if they had parachuted to safety.

The days we spent at Marigny were busy ones. We had to carry wounded men from an evacuation hospital all the way to the beachhead, a driving distance of eighty-five miles to the

Moving into Marigny. Note hole in steeple. An eighteen-year-old girl sniper killed by artillery shell from tank.

north. On these runs, we had to drive through St. Lo, and along the main thoroughfare was a narrow strip just wide enough for two vehicles to pass each other. On both sides lay the rubble and in the background the partly standing walls of the bombed buildings. It was a shame that this city had to suffer such destruction, but the Germans were stubbornly holding onto St. Lo. Only the mass bombing that took place on one of the days we were staying at Airel paved the way for the breakthrough that followed and liberated most of France. Underneath these ruins lay the bodies of many Germans who stubbornly held the city and had caused the 29th Infantry Division to suffer enormous casualties. Very few of the original division that landed on the beachhead remained with their units. We passed by the area where General McNair's coffin was placed on a hillside of rubble not long after he was killed. It was draped with an American flag and remained there for several hours to signify that he also gave his life in the battle for St. Lo.

After several trips back to the beachhead, we rested for several days at Marigny. Then, on August 1, our ambulance was called on to go up to the front. This was going to be our first experience on the front line, and we didn't have any idea of what it was like, but we were soon to find out. The ambulances of the Third Armored 45th Medical Battalion of the Third Armored Division had to go back to a maintenance outfit for repairs and checks, and we were chose to replace them for a short period.

We traveled in convoy to a clearing station, Company A of the 44th Medics, still in the thirty-mile-wide stretch in which the First and Third Armies rushed southward, we noticed that the terrain was changing. From the beach, we had passed through the hedgerows; then, down to this area, we had traveled over

41

flat land and now we were entering hilly country, the hills of Normandy. After receiving instructions at the clearing station, five of our ambulances were sent to a relay post. The other five, including mine, were forwarded to another. We had been driving on main asphalt roads up until now, and this relay post was on a dusty gravel road. We parked on a hillside and heard the tanks firing about two miles away. We could also see German 88 mm shells exploding in the air above a town about a mile from us. The Germans were timing their shells so that they would explode as air bursts. We were approximately four miles from a village called Mortain that the Germans were holding.

We remained at the relay post that night. After digging slit trenches and lining them with blankets, we crawled in. There wasn't too much noise from the guns, and since I was accustomed to sleeping on the ground by now, I had no trouble going to sleep. The next morning, Lemons and I were assigned to a first-aid station. The gravel road was dusty, as there were many 2 1/2-ton quartermaster trucks carrying up some supplies to the Third Armored Division. We had been given a map, but because of the dusty conditions in following the trucks, it was hard to see where we were going. As we drove along in #11, we looked through the dust on both sides of the road for the first-aid station. We had been told that it was a tent twenty feet by twenty feet with a large red cross on it. We passed several tanks that were camouflaged but didn't see a tent anywhere. The dust cleared, and we started up a hill. Just as we got to the top and were ready to drive around a curve, we came to one of our tanks parked on the side of the road with its gun pointed toward the curve. The tank men stopped us and told us not to go any farther because a quarter of a mile down the road a German 88 mm was pointed at the curve and ready to blast anything that came around it. We thanked them for the warning and told them what we were looking for. They told us the first-aid station was back by the tanks we had just passed. We turned around, drove back to the tanks, and found out why we had not seen the tent – it had been dismantled. We were directed to the trucks belonging to the first-aid station.

We were attached to a Third Armored Task Force that had been resting and receiving supplies. We filled #11's gas tank and were prepared for the takeoff. For dinner, we had K rations. About three o'clock in the afternoon, we began to move. A truck or a vehicle was placed between each tank, so Lemons and I in #11 were sandwiched between too big tanks. As we traveled over the dusty roads, it was really a test of driving, as the tank in front of us would occasionally stop short and suddenly loom up in the dust in front of us. We would also have to stop short and hope that the tank in back would see us in time. It was difficult to see the road itself through so much dust. We were heading eastward but suddenly switched to the north. I lost all sense of direction but knew that our purpose was to circle around and trap the Germans. The 30th Infantry Division had secured the front along the thirty-mile stretch through which we had traveled, and the British were to come down from the north above and east of Mortain to meet us, thus trapping the Germans in a large pocket. However, at this time, the Germans had a slight advantage over us. They commanded several hills and could see everything we were doing and every move we made. They were blasting away at anything on the move.

We were moving fast in the dust, and it was difficult to know where the tank ahead of me was when suddenly it stopped and loomed up in front of me. I slammed my brakes down as far as I could and stopped. Just about that time, the tank behind #11 came up behind us. He used his brakes, but the tank tracks bumped #11 in the rear and bounced us into the tank in front of us. I got out and checked for damage. There was none, but between my ambulance and both tanks there were only about twelve inches to spare. Jokingly, I asked the tank driver if he had any liability insurance.

The column stopped for a brief period long enough for the dust to settle, which was a temporary relief. Suddenly, above us, we heard a roar and got a quick glimpse of a German Messerschmitt 109 zooming by just above the treetops. Almost immediately, and also barely missing the trees, came a U.S. Lockheed P-38 right on the 109's rear and blasting away at him with his machine guns. We never found out whether he shot the German down or not.

We began to move again. Even though our windows were closed, we still swallowed dust. The crosses on #11 were almost covered with it. Then, to our relief, we pulled out onto a paved road and advanced northward to a point about a mile and a half from a town called Barenton. Suddenly, in the woods behind a field by the side of us, we heard a loud explosion. As I looked in that direction, I saw a door blasted off a vehicle that was parked there. It flew up into the air about fifteen feet and came back down. Lemons and I, like all the others except the tank men, sprang from our vehicles and hit the ground. Then some of the armored infantrymen who were riding on the tanks moved cautiously over to the wrecked vehicle. It must have been an explosive preset so it would go off several hours later with the hopes that it might kill a few Americans.

The signal came to move again. We had just driven a short distance when, about a half-mile from the town, the front of the column met some more resistance. The first-aid station vehicles pulled into a field on the east side of the road next to a wooded area. The men set up the tent and placed the equipment in it. They signaled us to come in and park next to the woods. Lemons and I immediately dug our slit trenches, this time a little deeper. Since the Germans were rooted in Barenton, we were expecting casualties. It was almost dark now and there was a red glow in the sky above the town. Lemons and I covered #11 with a camouflage net because on the south side of our field there were three seventy-five howitzer light tanks with short-nosed cannons. They were facing the enemy, and occasionally they would open fire and send 75 mm shells over to the enemy side.

Shortly after dark, several bombers came over, dropped flares, and brightened up the entire area. They waited for antiaircraft fire so they could bomb these positions, hoping they would be able to make a few strikes. No one opened fire on them, and they left without dropping any bombs. Covered with branches and a net, the red crosses on #11 were not visible. However, the red cross on the tent stuck out like a sore thumb. Seeing the red cross no doubt and not seeing anything else that was camouflaged and hidden might have helped them to come to their decision.

The casualties began to come in, and soon there were enough for a trip back to the clearing station. I considered this would be a difficult trip. I wondered if I could find the way back. Since we traveled in dust most of the time, it was almost impossible to observe any of our surroundings as we traveled and memorize the appearance of any buildings or other things in our minds so that we could recognize them on the return trip. We had the maps, but with total darkness and not being allowed to use headlights, the charts were useless. We had small lights in front like cat's eyes, but these were only for the benefit of approaching vehicles, and even then, they could barely be seen. So it meant driving in darkness and riding on the same dusty roads, which we had driven on that afternoon in our mad rush to encircle the area held by the Germans.

We started on our way and found that driving on the paved road wasn't too bad. In the darkness, we could make out building and scenery we had passed. Our trouble began when we came up behind a column of vehicles and had no alternative but to follow slowly behind them. We could tell by the rumble that they were tanks and we figured we would have to follow them back through the dusty roads, adding to the difficulties we were already facing. Peering through the darkness, it looked like a dead end ahead, as nothing could be seen but trees in the background against the dark sky. I remembered that we had come out of the dusty road onto the paved road, so when the tanks made a right turn, we were almost at the trees, so I made the turn with them. We drove up a gravel road for about a tenth of a mile when the tanks ahead of us stopped. Since they had been on the road the task force had traveled over, I assumed these were American tanks. I was soon to find out differently.

I decided to check with the tank men and see if they could help me to find out where the clearing station was. As I stepped out of #11, I heard a familiar language that was spoken by some of the German families back home. I froze in my steps. I knew then that I was behind an enemy tank column. I eased back into #11 and told Lemons and the men. The men had turned all their weapons in before they left their outfits, and if we were captured, the Germans would have been required to treat us as prisoners of war according to the rules of warfare. The only trouble with that was that since the Germans were almost surrounded, as prisoners of war we would be facing a terrific shelling by our own guns.

One of the men in the back of our ambulance was a colonel. He told us to remain still, so we sat there almost breathless. We waited to see what they were going to do. If they started to turn around, I was going to turn around also. If I could get turned around toward the paved road, I was going to step on the accelerator and drive fast enough to create a dust screen, then rush back to the task force and report it. We waited. Finally, to our relief, the tanks began to move forward again. As they disappeared over a hill, I eased #11 backward until we were again on that paved road.

We had passed a small dirt road shortly before, so I drove back to it and backed into it. It wasn't very long until daylight. With unanimous agreement, we decided to stay there until it brightened enough to see where we were going. When dawn began to appear, we eased out and moved up the road slowly, hoping we wouldn't run into the Germans again. We realized that the next time might not be as fortunate for us as the first.

When we came up to the trees again, I noticed another gravel road on the far side of a building. It was larger than the one the tanks went up, but we didn't see it in the darkness. We finally arrived at the clearing station and reported the incident. We learned that five German tanks that had come over into our lines had been destroyed. I figured then that these must have been the ones we were following.

Lemons and I returned to the first-aid station. It was now well into the morning and we had no trouble returning. But when we arrived, we did run into danger. We had just covered up the ambulance with our net when things began to get "hot." The Germans began to counterattack and, in an attempt to cut us into two sections and isolate us on the south side, were trying to cut through the thirty-mile-wide strip the First and Third Armies had come through. They were moving a fresh panzer divisor through the narrow strip they had left to them between the British and us. Success would have been costly to us. The panzer division had only one road left to come through, and the entire division was driving along this road in a continuous column. Typhoons of the RAF and Thunderbolts of the U.S. Air Force went in to attack. They were firing rockets that were attached to the undercarriages of the planes. At the end of the day, almost all of the tanks and vehicles were destroyed.

Our trouble began when our reconnaissance planes were reporting enemy positions on the hills around Mortain, our tanks would zero in on the Germans. Our tanks in our field were firing as well and the enemy could see the smoke as the shells left. Then they would fire on our positions, 88 mm shells whistling in. Several landed in our field, and more than once, as Lemons and I hugged the bottom of our slit trenches, we received a dirt bath. None of the shells made direct hits on our tanks or vehicles. However, as I checked on #11 later, I noticed a small shrapnel hole in the lower part of the body just in front of the rear left fender.

The shelling slowed down as our fighter-bombers forced the Germans to their foxholes, but that night they stepped up their shelling again. It seemed like this night was the longest night we had spent in our lives. We prayed for day to come so that the P-47 fighters would return and drive the Germans back to shelter. Daylight finally did come, but it turned out to be just as bad, if not worse.

Before our fighters arrived, a flight of 109's flew in and strafed the field we were in. The tanks were camouflaged, and they may not have seen them, but several times the bullets ripped into the ground close enough to cause us to get showered with chunks of dirt again. Several times during the day, when our fighters were not around, they returned and strafed our field.

During these strafings, I witnessed something I will never forget. As we lay in our slit trenches, a Jewish medical officer — a captain whose name I cannot remember — was attending to a sergeant who had a large hole in his head about the size of a baseball. All the time during the strafings, he stood in the tent whistling as if nothing out of the ordinary was happening. His calmness helped to strengthen us during the attacks.

The German counterattack was unsuccessful and, realizing the trap they were being drawn into, they began to retreat. The British advanced down to a town called Falaise as our task force and several others moved northward. We passed through Argentan and were closing in with a gap left of only six miles between us and the British. The Germans were fighting hard to keep it open.

It was during this time in our bitter advance northward from Argentan that our company suffered its first fatality. One of our first-aid men, traveling at the head of our task force, went to the aid of a wounded German who was yelling for help. As he bent down over the German to examine him, the Nazi rose up and stabbed him with a bayonet, killing him instantly. Several infantrymen saw what happened, opened up on the German with their Browning automatic rifles, and riddled him with bullets. The medic was pronounced dead by the medical officer of the first-aid station. My heart was sick, and I had an empty feeling in my stomach as I looked at him.

As the U.S. and British forces closed in, they had to be careful not to fire on each other, but they finally closed the gap and trapped 60,000 Germans and a countless number of vehicles in a large pocket. Almost immediately, three task forces turned and began advancing on main roads toward Paris.

On August 13, the Third Armored ambulances returned to their outfits, thus relieving us from the task force along with our other ambulance drivers. Several of our ambulances suffered damage. Yehle's ambulance #12 was hit; and Able's ambulance #15 was struck. They were hit by shrapnel and damaged seriously enough to have to be sent to ordinance for repairs.

We were bivouacked in a field just outside a town called Brecey. This town had suffered very little damage, and it seemed peaceful and quiet here. Lemons and I had become experts in digging slit trenches, and in just a few moments, we had our beds for the night dug out and lined with blankets. Darkness came, and we lay down to sleep. The peace and quiet of this town didn't last too long, however. Several German bombers flew over and dropped a few "eggs" on the town. Some of the bombs landed in our field and killed five cows. Things got quiet again, and we finally went off to sleep.

In the morning, when I awoke, I discovered I had almost shared my slit trench with a dead cow. Just a few feet more and the cow would have landed on top of my trench. As I looked over the situation later, I was relieved that this had not occurred, but wondered whether I would have been able to crawl out of my slit trench with a dead cow on top.

The next several days were peaceful and uneventful ones. I dug another slit trench in a more pleasant location and had several nights of much-needed rest. The meals at the company kitchen were a welcome change from the K rations we had to eat for several days, as there had been no time at all for the armored outfits to set up their kitchens. Our company meals were made from C rations, but even then, we would yearn for a good home-cooked meal. The C rations came in large cans — about one-half gallon size — and were served hot, so at least they tasted like a meal. However, the only eggs for breakfast in the morning were powdered eggs, which weren't very tasty and were a poor substitute for the real ones.

Since we had landed, we had begun to pick up a few French words and were able to communicate with the French civilians enough to trade some cigarettes for eggs or other things. Occasionally, we would cook a fried egg in our mess kits. I longed for some German fried pancakes that my mother made, usually on Fridays. It had been several years since I had eaten any, and it was one of my favorite meals. I had watched her make them and fry them and had a good idea of how to mix up the batter. So one afternoon, after making a trade with a French farmer for some potatoes and eggs, I begged a little flour and lard from the cooks, scalded my steel helmet, mixed up a pancake batter in it, and began to fry pancakes in my mess kit over a small stereo stove. It wasn't long before the rest of the ambulance section smelled the aroma. They came over like a pack of wolves, and I spent about two hours frying pancakes until the potatoes and eggs were used up. When I got to the last pancake, I was ready to fight for it. I was determined to get at least one out of the deal! By that time, they were well satisfied, and no one else came around.

On August 15, our company moved to the city of Sees, about seven miles south of Argentan. Here our ambulances worked with an 80th Infantry Division clearing station for several days. We carried wounded men back to an evacuation hospital. British and American "mop up" forces were knocking out the resistance in the pocket while the other American forces were racing toward Paris.

Relieved from the 80th, five of our ambulances — including #11 — were sent to work with a Ninth Armored Division clearing station. Here most of our patients consisted of German wounded who were left in the pocket. Twenty thousand Germans managed to escape from the pocket, but forty thousand others were taken as prisoners, and many of these were in critical condition.

At this time, the First and Third Armies were advancing so quickly, C-47 transport planes had to be used to transport gasoline and supplies to the fast-speeding columns. The entire front was now fluid, and some of the papers back home read as their headline, "Where is Patton?" The First Army was getting close to Paris, and General Patton's Third Army was racing across France far south of the city without any opposition at all.

On August 22, we transferred over and became attached to the 90th Infantry Division clearing station and traveled with them to Fontainebleau, thirty-two miles south of Paris. I had hoped that I would see the big city since I had heard so much about it. Now it looked as if I were going to miss it, as Patton was far to the east now and getting close to the border of

France and Germany. However, on August 23, my hopes revived, as our ambulance platoon was relieved from the 90th Division clearing station, and we joined the 28th Infantry Division clearing station at Ramboulet, twenty miles southwest of Paris.

Because of the beauty of the city and the fast advance of the Allied forces, the Germans announced that they would withdraw from it and declare Paris an open city. This meant we could enter without contest, and they would withdraw several miles to the north. Their plan was probably to reorganize and make a stand somewhere to the east.

THE LIBERATION OF PARIS

August 26 was one of the big days we were looking for. The 28th Infantry Division swung around the city and a French armored division, one that had escaped from France at Dunkirk during the Nazi onslaught in 1939, pulled in front of the city and was the first of the liberation forces to enter. Then various elements of the Allied forces — including the 28th Infantry Division clearing station medics — entered.

Our ambulance platoon followed them in convoy as they began the march along the Avenue des Champs-Élysées. What a sight! Tears of joy were flowing freely as the French civilians swarmed all over our ambulances. It was almost impossible to drive. We had to inch our way through, and at times when we were forced to stop, we were showered with kisses not only by the girls but the men, women, and children. For almost five years, these people had been under German domination. Now they were liberated, and it was impossible for them to control their emotions. Such a display of joy stirred us considerably. Not even New York on New Year's Eve one second before midnight and as the New Year rolled in could be compared to the event that was taking place during these moments. No doubt there were plenty of reunions as the French soldiers who hadn't seen their loved ones in years spotted them in the crowds. There was some sadness also as the soldiers learned that some of their relatives had been killed by the Nazis.

It took us a few hours to drive along the Avenue des Champs-Élysées, around the Arc de Triomphe and through the rest of the city. Toward evening, the clearing station set up its

Church of the Sacre Coeur, August 1944

Arc de Triomphe, August 1944

tents on the outskirts of the northeastern section of the city because the Germans were putting up some resistance twelve miles to the northeast of us. The 28th Infantry Divisions was already engaged in combat with them. Casualties were coming in, and it wasn't long before we had to make a trip back through the city. We did not have a map, and I knew it would be difficult to find our way back through Paris as it was now dark and we had to take a different route to get to the other side of Versailles where an evacuation hospital was set up. The layout of the streets was somewhat like the spokes of a wheel with the hub being the Arc de Triomphe and a main thoroughfare circling the outer section of the city. From the Eiffel Tower, it would look like a huge wheel with the Arc de Triomphe in the center.

Lemons and I drove back down one of these streets, and when we came to the Arc de Triomphe, we had difficulty finding the street that we were supposed to take to get back to Versailles. I drove around the Arc several times; the streets all looked alike. We finally spotted a French policeman and managed to make him understand we wanted to know the way back to Versailles. He put us on the right street.

As we drove along, we heard an occasional shot. In spite of the fact that the Germans declared it an open city, they left quite a few snipers. The FFI (Free French of the Interior), an underground civilian organization that worked secretly against the Germans, were engaged in searching out these snipers. It was quite dangerous for us while we were traveling at night. We managed to get through the city and find our way to the evacuation hospital to drop off our patients. By that time, it was daylight. When we started back through the city, it was bustling with activity. We found a bookshop and stopped for a few minutes to buy a map of Paris with the French money we were given in place of American money. Picking up a few French words here and there and occasionally meeting someone who understood a little English was making it easier to communicate with the French. However, the girl who sold me the map spoke perfect English. She had spent several years living in New York City and sounded more American than French.

We made another trip through Paris that day, and with the map, it was a cinch. We were also beginning to recognize our surroundings. However, the danger was still there. We saw a free Frenchman shot and killed by a sniper. Other members of the Free French of the Interior closed in on the snipe, and without a doubt, he was also killed. The FFI were jittery; they didn't trust anyone, especially at night when they were patrolling the streets. They checked all vehicles, and as we came through on the night of August 27 on another run back to the hospital, they stopped us. One of the FFI walked up to the side of ambulance #11 and pointed a machine gun at the side of my head. As he spoke to me, another one lurked by the side of his car ready to shoot us. I showed him my medical identification card, and after he looked and saw the wounded on litters, he seemed to be convinced that we were Americans. He shook my hand and told us to go on. As I left, I breathed a sigh of relief. After all, it wasn't a very good feeling to have the barrel of a small machine gun pointed at my temple.

The next day, as we traveled through Paris, we witnessed an event that was taking place in many of the cities as each of them was liberated. The FFI were marching young women up the street to a well-crowded section. Here they shaved the hair off their heads, stripped them of their clothing, and made them run home in shame. These women had become extra friendly with the Germans and were now paying for their evil deeds.

The 28th Infantry Division, along with armored units, wiped out the resistance and on August 29, we advanced with the 28th clearing station to a point twenty miles northeast of Paris. We parked in a field next to the clearing station. The job of digging a slit trench was unnecessary sometimes as there seemed to be plenty of them available in places where we bivouacked. The medics looked for a place that had previously been occupied by other American units, thus reducing the danger of a hidden booby trap or mine. When we were pretty far from the front, and it seemed peaceful, we would sleep on litters in #11 at night. We would set up the two litters on the ambulance floor and line them with blankets.

It wasn't dark yet, so I set about my almost daily job of writing to my wife and family back in the States. Bevin Circle Eagle, a full-blooded Sioux and a good friend of mine, borrowed a mirror from me and was shaving at the back of #11. Suddenly, we heard a strange noise, a sound we had never heard before. Lemons and I got out of #11 and looked up in the sky. We all saw a strange-looking plane coming toward us from the northeast. As it finally passed over our heads, we noticed a trail of fire shooting out from behind it. Seven times that night, we awoke to the sound of one of these strange planes.

Hitler boasted of a secret weapon, and this was it — a robot plane propelled by a rocket with a built-in bomb. We began to call them "buzz bombs." We also heard Hitler was sending V-1 rocket bombs over to London, England. These were held by a ramp, and when they went off, they shot miles into the air before dropping somewhere in London.

We spent several days here until the Germans again began to retreat. On September 2, the 28th clearing station advanced to a town called Chauny. As we traveled with the medical outfit in our ambulances, we passed several burned-out German tanks that were still smoldering. Dead horses, which had been pulled to the side of the road, were still warm. The civilians told us that the Germans had left only a few hours before.

Since the closing days of July, we had been moving forward at a fast pace. It now appeared as if the Germans were going to give up not only France but Belgium, Holland, and Luxembourg as well and retreat back behind their own border and probably make a stand at the Siegfried Line.

After traveling with the 28th Infantry medical clearing station for about two weeks, we left them and rejoined the rest of our company at Charleville, near the border of France and Belgium. They were ready to move when we joined them, so we started northward. We passed through Sedan, passing by trenches that were dug during World War I and left as landmarks and memories of the past conflict. As we passed them, I said to Lemons, "Here we are back in the same place and fighting the same enemy our country fought twenty-seven years ago." I thought of the men I had seen back home who had fought in that war and remembered the condition some of them were in because of the poison gas that was used, probably at this exact spot. The war we were engaged in now was bad enough, but so far, either side had not used poison gas. We had received training, however, on how to recognize different kinds of gases, and gas masks were part of our equipment.

After leaving Sedan, we passed through the Maginot Line fortifications that were supposed to have been impregnable but had been easily penetrated by the Germans when they smashed into France. The Maginot Line had been built across France in front of the Belgian border, also — not because the French feared attack from Belgium, but just in case the Germans decided to attack France by overrunning Belgium and by passing the fortifications between France and Germany. However, the Nazis overran Holland, Belgium, and France, holding territory from the southwest part of France eastward to the west end of their own nation up until the invasion of Normandy.

BELGIUM

We entered Belgium and bivouacked at the small town called Newfontaine. Here we rested for a few days while we waited for another assignment. The First Army was still advancing in a northeasterly direction, while General Patton's Third Army had already penetrated the Siegfried Line defenses inside Germany but had to withdraw because of an inability to get enough gasoline and supplies fast enough. The quartermaster supply trucks were running twenty-four hours back and forth, but it was impossible to supply every unit daily, especially the fast-moving ones that were requiring gasoline and oil continuously. By the time the needed supplies came forward, the Germans had time to reorganize and entrench themselves in the fortifications and build up a strong resistance. General Hodge's First Army had advanced to within seven miles of Aachen, Germany, which was about ten miles northeast of Eupen, Belgium.

The 451st Medical Collecting Company was proving itself a worthy and dependable outfit. We were kept as close to the front line as possible, so in just a few days we moved again, this time to Bastogne. This was a quiet town in Belgium, and because of the quick retreat of Germans, it suffered very little damage. The first few evenings we walked to the village, which was about a half mile from the field we bivouacked in. The Belgian people spoke the French language, so we communicated with them enough to greet them and sometimes trade for eggs. Our meals were much better now than when we had first landed in France, but we still had powdered eggs for breakfast. Whenever we could, we would trade with the local civilians for some "chicken fruit." We didn't complain about the powdered eggs because we knew that was the only kind of eggs that could be shipped to us, but real eggs were a treat when we could trade for them. The Belgian people were very friendly, and they were glad to see us there.

For the ambulance platoon, our stay Bastogne was very short. We left the company after being ordered to the southeast to work with the Fourth Infantry medical clearing station about one-half mile inside the German border and just north of the nation of Luxembourg. Lemons worked with another driver temporarily, as Lieutenant Brehem, our ambulance platoon leader was riding with me. We were on a special detail. We had to travel through a small town called St. Vith, another beautiful village with old but well-kept buildings and homes. This town was also unharmed by the horrors of war, but the local residents little knew what the future had in store for them.

We crossed the border and drove into the field where the medical clearing station was set up. We parked in front of the receiving tent, and after having supper, we came back to ambulance #11. Since it was quite foggy in this area, and there wasn't much to do, we decided to retire before dark. It was around nine p.m. when we prepared our litters for the night's rest.

About ten minutes after we had lain down, I heard voices. The lieutenant had already gone to sleep; I tried to call him softly, but he didn't hear me. The voices were those of Germans, and as I raised my head and looked toward the front of the ambulance, I saw someone crouched down. We kept the doors to #11 locked when we slept in it, so I was thankful for that. The German came around to the driver's side and attempted to look in. however, at this time, it was too dark to see anything inside our ambulance, so he couldn't see us lying on the litters. I lay motionless and wondered what they would have done if they had seen us in the ambulance or if they thought we might have seen them.

Road in Bulge area

Finally, the group moved away and after a few moments, when I figured they were out of hearing distance, I woke up the lieutenant and told him about it. We got out of #11 and looked around and listened, but the fog was so thick we couldn't even see the receiving tent. The lieutenant told me to notify the guards. With a rifle pointed at me, I first identified myself and then told the guard what had happened. He, in turn, called the sergeant of the guard who then searched the area with several others. I went back to the ambulance, locked the doors, and finally went to sleep.

In the morning, when the lieutenant and I talked about it, we assumed it must have been a German scout patrol that had crossed the Siegfried Line fortifications about a quarter of a mile away. They must have traveled quite a few miles, as some of our First Army units were several miles inside of Germany.

The next day, as the fog cleared and the sun came out, I could see shells exploding on hills to the east. Occasionally, a column of black smoke would ascend into the sky, indicating a building or a vehicle or something else had been destroyed. As I watched, our P-47 Thunderbolts appeared and began to dive bomb on German positions. German antiaircraft batteries were firing up at them, and as each plane dived, I held my breath and hoped the pilot would pull out of the dive before he got hit with ground fire.

When it was quiet, I caught up on my letter writing, shaved, and rested, as there wasn't much for me to do. The lieutenant was on liaison duty at the clearing station, and occasionally we would make a trip. I was not carrying casualties at this time, just driving the lieutenant around when necessary. At night, I went to the recreation tent and watched a movie, but I always had to let the lieutenant know where I would be in case he needed me.

Our company was ordered to move to Eupen, Belgium, on September 25. We returned to Bastogne, and soon were on our way. It was a seventy-five-mile trip. We traveled through Liege and several cities or towns. When we arrived at Eupen, we moved into a field with the 45th Evacuation Hospital. Several days later, the evacuation hospital moved into a large building that the Belgians turned over to us to use. The building itself was either a school or a hospital. The reception room looked like a gymnasium. We moved into a field behind this building, but it began to rain. The field became muddy, so our officers moved us into vacant houses that the Germans had left. We were crowded in, however, so some of us slept in our ambulances at nights, letting the others have more room between their cots. Since we were used to it, we didn't mind it anyway. Our ambulances were parked in a grassy field across from the house we were using.

We noticed a difference in this city; the people didn't seem to be as friendly as the civilians in other parts of Belgium. Maybe it was just city life itself. I remembered back home when, during the first twelve years of my life, our family lived in New York City and everyone seemed so busy they didn't have time to associate with their neighbors. We lived next door to neighbors for seven years before we became acquainted with them. But when we moved out on Long Island to Medford, the neighbors seemed closer together and had more time for fellowship with each other. These people of Eupen didn't seem to appreciate their liberation as the people of Paris did. Besides that, half of them spoke two languages — German and French. Because of that, there was an excellent opportunity for German agents to be disguised among them, and there may have been some fear existing among the local civilians. So, we were warned to be careful if we got into a conversation with them, as we might be talking to a German spy.

We started to use a password each day when we entered the hospital. We used it traveling on the road as well. A new word came down each day directly from Supreme Headquarters. Anyone in an American uniform who didn't know

German tank destroyed at Eupen, Belgium, October 1944

Wrecked buildings in Eupen

the password was detained and checked out before he was released.

One morning, about a week after we had arrived at Eupen, we we're still sleeping in our ambulances when we heard a strange noise again and recognized it as the noise we had heard around Paris. Yehle and I jumped out of our ambulances at the same time, looked up, and saw a buzz bomb pass over us. From then on, they began to fly over quite frequently. Sometimes they came over in threes, almost side by side. Many of them crashed on the city of Liege. For military purposes, they were of no value, as the Germans had no control over them after they left the ramp. Most of them wrecked homes and killed civilians or crashed in fields, exploding without harm. Their main purpose was the put fear into the civilian population and cause panic. Then, too, a lucky hit might knock out an American vehicle or installation. It did become a little bothersome, as many of them dropped around us. The Germans began to send over so many that we began to call the area we were now in "Buzz Bomb Alley." Most of them were sent over at night, but also on cloudy days, many came over. The Germans had their ramps well hidden, and it was hard for our fighter-bombers to locate the launching sites. The ramps were nothing but railroad tracks that ran about a quarter of a mile, and then curved up at about forty-five degrees toward the sky. We would watch them as they came over, and if the noise stopped and the flame went out as it was approaching, we jumped into a hole like prairie dogs because we knew it was on a downward path. After they passed over, we usually watched the fiery trails until they were out of sight.

The buzz bombs were too fast for our planes, but our P-51 Mustangs could catch up with them on a dive. One day, we saw a Mustang dive down at one and strafe it, and it exploded in the air.

Hitler must have known my birthday was November 5, because on that morning, as I got ready to start my ambulance and drive down to the evacuation hospital to pick up a load of patients and carry them back to a station hospital, I heard a buzz bomb approaching. As I looked up and saw it coming, the noise suddenly stopped and it began its descent. It appeared as if it were coming straight at me. I nosedived into a slit trench close to #11 and waited, almost breathless. I just knew that thing was coming into my slit trench but was relived when I heard the wind whistle overhead. I jumped up and watched then after it had passed about fifty feet above me. We were parked on a hill, and I was able to watch it as it just missed the 45th Evacuation Hospital and slammed into a building in Eupen and exploded. Bricks, debris, and smoke went up into the air. We didn't find out if there were any casualties from that one, but I always called it "my birthday present from Hitler."

I had just parked #11 one night, when I looked to the north and saw a fiery trail headed almost straight up into the sky. It looked like a skyrocket in the distance. We had heard about the V-1 bombs the Germans were sending over to England, but we had been too far south to see any of them. Now, we were in viewing distance as they traveled skyward. Each one, as it was launched, continued to go up until it went out of sight. These, too, were uncontrolled except that, through experience, they were able to drop each one somewhere within the city of London. Like the buzz bombs, these were used to create a nerve-racking effect on the British civilians.

Leuck, with Ambulance #14, looking over a smashed German vehicle, November 1944

The city of Aachen was finally taken after much blood was shed. Not a thing was left but a mass of walls standing up. The Germans retreated to Duren, Germany, where they decided to make another stand. It appeared as if we were to be stalled at the Siegfried Line for the winter. Rainy weather was appearing quite constantly. The warm, dry season was over, and it was beginning to grow colder each day. Frost had already appeared, and the men at the front were having mud problems. They were also having problems with exhaustion. Many of them had been up at the front for a long time now without being relieved. Some of the supplies grew scare, causing morale to sink. They were complaining about not getting enough cigarettes and other personal necessities. We heard that there was a black market going on in Paris, and some enlisted men

70

had already been caught and court-martialed. Whenever we had the opportunity, we would send whatever surplus cigarettes, razor blades, or personal articles we had available with the ambulance drivers coming in from the clearing stations. Sometimes when we went up to the clearing stations, we would carry whatever we could and forward them on from there. Occasionally, we would drive up to clearing stations when they became filled up and would transport exhaust patients to an exhaustion center in a town called Herhesthal, some to an exhaustion center in Malmedy, Belgium, thirty miles to the south, and other to a convalescent hospital in Maastricht, Holland.

Hospital grounds at Brand near Aachen

To get to Germany, sometimes we would travel through the small nation of Luxembourg, which had been a neutral nation but had been taken over by the Germans. It suffered little damage. Other times we would pass through a stretch of land that would carry us through three nations in less than ten minutes. From Belgium, we would cross the border into Germany and a few minutes later, into Holland.

On one of these trips, Lemons and I had another close call. In order to cross the border into Holland, we had to leave the highway, which was bombed at the border, and drive #11 through a field. Some of the Siegfried Line defenses had been knocked out of the way, enough of them to allow a vehicle to pass through. Sometime during the night, a German agent had planted a mine in the improvised road. Just before we arrived there, an army jeep started through and was blown up, the two soldiers in the jeep being killed. We had to wait about ten minutes until a demolition squad checked the area. Then we were allowed to pass through with our load of patients and go on to the convalescent hospital. We were able to drive up far enough into Holland to see and take pictures of some of the windmills. I was fortunate enough to be able to purchase a small pair of wooden shoes, which I shipped home to my little ten-year-old sister-in-law. Also, on these trips into Holland, we were again able to see the toll our American planes were taking on the German vehicles. On the side of the road lay an entire column of burned out tanks and trucks.

One afternoon around the middle of November, as we parked our ambulance back at Eupen, Lemons and I saw an army Piper Cub in trouble. The air force was using these small planes as artillery spotters. In case of trouble, they could land quickly in a small amount of space. The pilot of the Cub was

Dutch home in Holland

flying back to his base when an ME-109 German fighter came after him. Diving down, he strafed the smaller plane. The lieutenant crash-landed in our field but fortunately, escaped unhurt. The German fled as antiaircraft artillery opened fire on him. We walked the lieutenant to the evacuation hospital where they checked him for possible injuries. When they found him okay, we carried him to his unit.

There must have been a large concentration of our forces around Eupen because the Germans were trying to make it "hot" for us. In addition to the buzz bombs, they moved a large railroad gun in somewhere close to Aachen. It had a long-distance range, and they kept it well camouflaged. Just as soon as darkness came, they would fire shells in Eupen, each shell about fifteen minutes apart, continuing throughout the night. We just about knew when another one would come in. Some of them landed really close to us. In fact, one shell barely missed a civilian hospital south of the field our ambulances were parked in.

Stiffened resistance from the Germans kept us stalled just outside of Aachen and along the entire line. November passed, and the month of December brought bitterly cold weather. The First Army had dug in between Aachen and Duren in the Hürtgen forest. Most of the patients we were bringing in from Germany now were being afflicted with trench foot, which was nothing but frostbite. Some of the men were affected so badly they had to have toes amputated. Their toes would freeze, the circulation would stop, and the toes would turn black. Nothing else could be done but to remove them.

Many of the GIs built small huts and made stoves out of empty oil drums. For heat, they used drained oil and scrap wood. This helped to slow down the casualties from frostbite. It

One of the assistant drivers as we entered Germany for
the first time, November 1944

was simple to build one of these huts, which were like log cabins, as there were plenty of logs around from the splintered trees. With a saw and a hammer, one of them could be built in a few minutes. The cracks were filled in with mud. They would cut a hole out of the side and top of a used oil drum, weld a stovepipe to the top hole, and it wouldn't be long until they had a warm hut. With the idea of having to stay until spring when the Allies could launch another offensive, the GIs built a log-cabin city in the forest.

On one of these cold days, I had my first problem with ambulance #11. We arrived at the clearing station in the Hürtgen forest and had to wait for a load of patients. About two hours later, Lemons and I started back with an ambulance load. The temperature was well below freezing, the roads were caked with snow and ice, the trees looked as though they were made of glass with their coating of ice, and heavy clouds darkened the sky. Not long after we left the clearing station, #11 began to stall. I would start it up, we would run a few feet, and the motor would quit again. It finally quit, and I couldn't crank it at all then. Here we sat for almost a half hour, and it began to get cold in the ambulance. Some of the men in back had frostbite. To add to the misery, we were in an isolated spot. Not a truck or vehicle came along during the time we were stranded. Even though I didn't have much confidence that I could get #11 started again, I decided to try once more after a while had passed. To our relief, it started. The motor had gotten warm enough to melt the ice in the fuel line. With no further trouble, we got back to Eupen, and I reported the problem to Sergeant Renfro, our staff sergeant in charge of the ambulance platoon. He poured a quart of alcohol in the gas tank, and I had no more gas problems. I must have gotten some gas with a little water in it.

Pillbox blown up outside of Aachen

Toward the middle of December, the Germans began to get daring. We didn't know it, but something was about to take place. The Luftwaffe began to attack in broad daylight. They had been coming out mostly at night to avoid engaging in battles with our Air Force since our planes had taken a serious toll on theirs. It was mostly fighters that would come in and strafe before fleeing back into Germany. It was more than we had seen in quite a while during the day, though. On one quiet Sunday afternoon, a number of them came over and strafed in several areas of Eupen. They didn't tarry long because, in just a short time, our Mustangs came to the scene in quick pursuit.

Our thoughts of being stalled for the winter didn't last long, as the Germans began an offensive on December 16. Hitler boasted that he would spend Christmas in Paris. The Germans had secretly brought up several reorganized panzer divisions under cover of the Hürtgen forest in the area close to Malmedy. Their plan was to attack swiftly, capture big gasoline dumps, and drive toward Antwerp and Belgium, thus cutting the Allied-occupied territory in two. Actually, no one believed they really thought they could do it, but figured it to be a last frantic attempt meant to build up the morale of the German people.

Malmedy was a weak point. It was held lightly since it was a mountainous area and an offensive was expected from there. General VonRunstedt struck from the east, however, and as he pressed forward, he didn't find the expected gasoline dumps. This slowed him down a little, as he had to get supplies from the rear.

Before dawn on the morning of December 16, when the Germans began their offensive, more shells came whistling into Eupen. At the same time, a number of bombers came over and began to drop heavy bombs on the city. Several of us stood in a five-feet-deep foundation close to the civilian hospital. They had dropped flares that lit up the city. Since we were on the hill overlooking the main district, we had an excellent view from our position. Some small incendiary bombs were used as well and one of them hit the house where part of our 451st Medical Collecting Company was lodging. The men quickly evacuated the building, none of them being injured. They put out the fire, which was hindered by the snow on the roof. Several times, the bombers flew directly over us, and we hugged the side of the little concrete pit a little closer. We could see the black crosses on the wings of the bombers as the flares slowly floated down beneath the planes. The sky was filled with thousands of tracer bullets and antiaircraft fire. Down went one of the bombers after exploding into a ball of flame. After a short period, the bombers flew away, but the shells continued to come in. the Germans must have brought up some more railroad guns. Hitler promised that he was going to flatten Eupen.

Our home at Eupen

THE JET

On the afternoon of the 16th, we heard a strange whistling noise, much different from the noise of the buzz bombs. Looking up over the civilian hospital in the direction it was coming from, I noticed a plane that was moving faster than any plane I had ever seen. It was moving so fast, I had to look ahead of the sound before I finally saw it. Then I remembered some rumors I had heard about a "jet" plane the Germans were boasting about. They had successfully installed a rocket engine in an aircraft. This was the plane, and it was on a reconnaissance mission, probably taking pictures of the damage the bombers and shells had done to Eupen. The antiaircraft artillery was firing at it, but the ack-ack was exploding well behind. If many of these showed up in the near future, it meant our gunners would have to learn to fire well in advance of these jets in order to make a strike.

The Germans began to infiltrate our lines using GI clothing. The passwords were now more important than ever. Their planes dropped several thousand storm troopers behind our lines in order to kill, disrupt communications, and cause confusion wherever they could. Since there was a curfew for the civilians and only army personnel were out at night and were expected to know the passwords, many of these paratroopers in American uniforms were captured.

Such was the case on the night of December 16. I was unloading a group of wounded men from #11 when a GI asked me which was it was to the street. It struck me the wrong way when he asked because I knew a wounded soldier would head into the receiving room of the hospital and not want to head for the street. I suspected something was wrong. It was dark, and I couldn't see if he had a medical tag hanging from him or not. As the curtain in front of the hospital entrance flipped open a little, I saw he was not wearing a tag. I saw his face, and he looked like a tall blonde German.

I had to think quickly. If I yelled for a guard, he might draw a gun and kill me and a few others around. I did the first thing that entered my mind. I knew there were a couple of guards at the entrance of the driveway exit, so I pointed in that direction, knowing that they would draw a gun on anyone who came along. They had been instructed to challenge every GI and vehicle that came in or out of the exit. As he walked toward the exit, I hoped the guards would be on the alert and not get shot. I knew that if he were a German, he wouldn't know the password and would be captured right there. I heard later that an SS paratrooper had landed on the hospital roof and was captured. It may have been he who might have come down from the roof and through the hospital, mingled with us, and then headed for the street. If it was he, he made his mistake by asking me how to get here.

The German panzer units were closing in on Malmedy, thirty miles to the south, and it appeared as if the city would be taken before enough units could arrive to defend it. Several evacuation hospitals were down there just east of the city, so every ambulance available was required to go down and evacuate the wounded immediately. Lemons and I received our orders and headed there immediately. It was December 17 when we drove through Malmedy and arrived at the hospital we were ordered to. Here I met Bill Hahn from my hometown of Medford once again. We didn't have but a second to greet each other when shells started to smash in. I got a load of patients and pulled out. Bill told me that a panzer task force was about a mile away.

As we left the area, we had to climb a hill. Already the Germans had their guns pointed at it. As we sped up the hill, several shells dropped too close for comfort, and #11 got a few shrapnel holes in the body. None of them came inside, though. We got up over the hill and were safe after that. Some of the wounded men in our ambulance said that they saw the tanks that were shooting at us down below about a mile from the hospital. We heard later that the hospital personnel barely got out. They had their personal equipment loaded on trucks, but had to abandon some of their medical equipment and supplies.

Everyone did not escape, however. The ambulance drivers and assistants of ten ambulances from the 575th Ambulance Battalion were captured. The SS troopers examined their ambulances, found guns and pistols that they had collected as souvenirs, and then lined the drivers up, and cut them down with machine guns. When I heard this, I shuddered to think of what could have happened to me, also, if I had been captured at Malmedy. I had a 32 automatic pistol hidden in my ambulance that I was keeping as a souvenir. When we returned to Eupen, I took it out, put it in my duffel bag, and left it at the house where we kept our personal belongings.

The day after we left Malmedy, we learned that the panzer units had smashed in and taken the city. An exhaustion station that was part of our 68th Medical Group had packed up and left the city a short time before. It was on the road in convoy with red crosses clearly showing when it was attacked and strafed by German fighters. Several of our officers and men were killed.

The Germans attacked St. Vith. The 106th Infantry Division held the town for several days but finally withdrew under a terrific pounding from German artillery. However, their heroic effort helped to slow the Nazi advance. The panzer units also converged on Bastogne, Belgium, where the 101st Airborne Division was holding the town. The 101st stubbornly held, and the Germans surrounded them. At one point, the German advance continued steadily but slowly for about one week until several American divisions rushed down from the Duren area and stopped them about two miles east of Marche.

After the enemy became stalled, they began to push to the right and left in pincer movements, as we had done east of St. Lo, but they were unsuccessful, and their big push turned into a bulge.

The panzer units were showing some strength east of the city of Eupen and were advancing towards this city. Besides the 45th Evacuation Hospital, there were several other army hospitals here. Since it was feared that Eupen might be taken, we all moved out. It was on Christmas morning when we left the city, our entire company heading southwest and settling down at the city of Huy, which was west of Liege. We had been promised a good Christmas dinner with turkey, stuffing, and all. About dinnertime, though, we were on the road. It tasted just as good on Christmas night at 7 p.m. as it would have at noon.

Some of our combat seasoned divisions that had been resting in the rear were brought up to the front, and the Germans were stopped at all points. Then the Nazis began to exert their pressure on the surrounded 101st Airborne Division at Bastogne. I didn't know it at the time, but one of my wife's cousins, James Bivvins, was a member of this division and was trapped in the city. General McAuliffe was the commander of

Wrecked building in Duren

the 101st, which was now taking a terrific pounding from German artillery. General Von Runstedt sent a party in with a white flag and demanded our forces to surrender. The reply that General McAuliffe gave made worldwide history when he said, "Nuts to you."

The Fourth and Seventh Armored Divisions began to attack from the south. The Second and Third Armored Divisions were preparing to attack but were slightly in the rear reorganizing and building back to full strength. Lemons and I joined the Third Armored 45th Medical Treatment Station, another frontline outfit at Darbry, a small, quiet, and peaceful town surrounded by mountains. The 45th was lodging in a castle at the edge of the small town. The castle was surrounded by a moat but had a concrete bridge instead of a drawbridge. It was normally being used as a convent, but the priests and nuns had moved out to let the Third Armored medics use it for a few days. Lemons and I slept in the castle at night on a nice soft bed in a room of our own. We felt like kings with the treatment we were receiving, the maids cleaning the room and changing the sheets daily.

Several days later, we were ready and on January 1, we pulled out. The Second and Third Armored Divisions began their attack from the north; the 28th, 104th, 30th, and the battered 106th Infantry Divisions attacked from the west. We pressed toward the besieged garrison at Bastogne as the Third Armored Division began the attack. To the left of us was the 83rd Infantry Division, and to the right was the Second Armored Division. The treatment station was set up at Werbomont, and we carried patients back to a medical clearing station.

Lemons and I were sent up to the first-aid station of the 83rd Armored Field Artillery Battalion. Their ambulance got a direct hit and was knocked out of service. We had gotten out of #11 and had entered a barn that the first-aid station was using when several shells came in. we hit the ground and one dropped real close and exploded, shaking the building. We lay on the straw almost breathless, wondering if one was going to hit the barn. The 83rd Field Artillery opened up, and for a few moments, there was an artillery duel, each side pouring it on the other. When it seemed as though the Germans quit firing in our direction, we walked outside to see if any damage was done. Ambulance #11 was hit; a truck was, also. The shell had exploded in front of the truck belonging to the first-aid unit, destroying the front end of it.

Ambulance #11 was out of running condition. It was riddled with shrapnel, the radiator was punctured, and antifreeze was running out on the snow. Three tires were punctured, and the body was full of holes. Our company was notified by radio to send up another ambulance, and, after a short while, #12 arrived. We stayed overnight, and here at the barn, we had another close one. We made beds out of the straw that was on the ground, covered it with a blanket, and lay down. It was cold, but we had plenty of blankets, and we finally drifted off to sleep. In the morning, when daylight came, one of the medics found an unexploded hand grenade hidden in the straw. After that, we began to search through all the straw. The search paid off as we found some wires. One end of them led to a detonator under the straw where I had been lying; the other end led to a five-pound charge of dynamite. From the detonator, the wires were connected to a battery, and from there, they continued on to the charge of dynamite. This made up an almost complete circuit, broken by the detonator only, which had a plunger on top of it. Had the plunger been pushed in, the circuit would have been completed, the charge would have gone off, and who knows what would have happened. It was a miracle that I hadn't set off the detonator when I lay down, as it was pushed down in the ground and the plunger end was sticking straight up. During the night, I had jerked suddenly when a gopher ran over my face and woke me up. Fortunately for us, the detonator must have been defective. We agreed that a knocked-out ambulance, a completely destroyed truck, rats running over our faces, and sleeping close to a death-dealing booby trap were enough trouble for one evening and night.

Up in the morning, our company maintenance truck came and towed ambulance #11 back to an ordinance unit for repairs. Lemons and I stayed back with the company at Huy for several days. One night, while we were there, we went to a U.S.O. show in which Marlene Dietrich was the main performer.

On January 5, we got #11 back. It looked like a brand new ambulance, just as we had seen it sitting in the field in Bristol, England. We were ordered back to frontline duty and sent to the Third Armored 45th Medical First Aid Station, which was getting ready to move. We traveled with them to Jevigne where they set up again. The Germans were now being driven back, the Second and Third Armored closing in on Bastogne from the north and the Fourth and Seventh Armored pushing up from the south. Finally, Patton's task forces broke through on the south end and rescued the 101st Airborne. The Third Armored broke through from the north, and the First and Third Armies were wiping out the bulge. Yehle's Ambulance #12 and Wilmes' Ambulance #16 had been working with other treatment stations, and both of them came back for repairs. They were full of shrapnel holes and needed body work. Ambulance #13, driven by Volz, and #14, driven by Leuck, turned over while trying to escape from shellfire, the shells landing close to them. Fortunately, they escaped without injury.

As we entered Bastogne, it was a different scene from when we had first entered it about five months ago. One building after another was heavily damaged by the shells the Germans had been firing into the city. The German army had been pulverizing the 101st Airborne. It must have been a shock to the Belgian civilians who had fled the city and were now returning to find it like this. When it had first been liberated, the damage had been slight. They thought the war was over for them, but now they would have to clear away the wreckage and rebuild. Many of them were probing around in what used to be their homes, trying to find some of their personal belongings.

We had a busy time here at Bastogne, as the casualties from the 101st were heavy, and we made a number of trips back and forth to the evacuation hospitals. The medical officers and nurses were working twenty-four hours or more without sleep until they became exhausted while trying to save the lives of some of the wounded from the 101st. We also had to make trips to a graves registration unit where we unloaded the dead.

When we finished carrying the casualties from Bastogne, we moved with the first-aid treatment station to a small village called Regne: This was on January 10, and here we encountered more danger. A medical truck belonging to the treatment unit we were with was just in front of us when it drove over a hidden mine and was blown up. The driver and his occupant were killed. Just as we pulled into a field, a jeep was blown apart by another hidden mine in the road. Lemons and I had passed over this mine just before we entered the field. No doubt, we had narrowly missed it.

I don't know how close we were to the Germans here, but I know we were too close for comfort. Our tanks close by were firing away, and shells were coming in, some of them really close to us. Again, we had to hope that one wouldn't come in that would take us out of this world. We were out in the open, the ground was frozen, and it was impossible to dig a slit trench. We had to "wear" it out. Finally, the enemy shelling stopped; our guns may have knocked out their artillery. It was still dangerous around here, and there were many hidden mines and booby traps around. The snow that was falling and that had already fallen helped to conceal them, so it made it impossible for the demolition units to find all of them.

There were a number of knocked-out German tanks here, and some of the men were looking into one of them. Curious like everyone else, Lemons and I walked over to it and looked in. propped up in the driver's seat was a dead German, frozen stiff. There were probably more in the other tanks, but we weren't anxious to move around too much, and we walked where there were footprints or vehicle tracks in the snow.

The time came to carry a load of wounded back to one of the clearing stations, so we loaded up and started on our way. In order to get out of this town, we had to climb a hill. The Germans had machine guns pointed at the top of it and were firing at everything that came over it. I drove back and told the medical officer I couldn't get over the hill until that machine gun nest was wiped out. The radio operator notified someone, and soon fire was concentrated on the area where the enemy fire was coming from. I drove off, sped up the hill, and got over the crest safely before another gunner could zero in on #11. On the return trip, we came over the hill fast but weren't fired upon. Our

A few of us drivers and our assistants at the church near
St. Vith, January 1945

American guns had probably run the Germans off or wiped them out.

We returned to the company on January 17, but we left again after two days. We went to work with the 82nd Airborne Division clearing station, which was set up not far from St. Vith in the Hürtgen forest. We were still experiencing bitter cold weather, the Germans were fighting furiously, and the casualties were heavy. Many were coming in with frostbite, along with the wounded in action. Our ambulance platoon was split up at the clearing station, and we were sent in pairs to various first-aid stations in the forest and west of St. Vith. Yehle and I were assigned together, each of us carrying a load of wounded back to the clearing station. That night, when we came back to the first-aid station, we slept in our ambulances. Lemons and I had plenty of blankets in the ambulance, but we still felt cold during the night. We could have slept warmed in a slit trench if we could have found one in the dark for each of us. During the night, when we finally did go off to sleep, we were occasionally awakened by artillery shells coming in. some of them came in close. When we checked our ambulances in the morning, we found some new holes from shrapnel in both ambulances. Fortunately, for us, the metal in the bodies of our ambulances kept us from being hit.

The next day we were relieved by two other ambulances, and we went back to join our ambulance section at the clearing station. It was outside of St. Vith, and we were using an abandoned church as the base from which we operated. We had heard that St. Vith had been leveled to the ground, and this was the only building that was intact, probably because it was slightly out of the main section, but even this had the windows blasted out of it. Looking toward St. Vith, we could not see the church steeples that we had seen several months before. We slept on the pews in the church that night but, with no windows, it was just like sleeping out in the open. The severe cold had broken a little, though, and with plenty of blankets, we slept comfortably. Even the sound of heavy artillery didn't bother us, nor did the occasional roar of an enemy plane flying overhead.

We were within walking distance of St. Vith's business area and main district, so after we had returned from a trip to a first-aid station one afternoon, Yehle and I decided to walk up to center of the town. When we got to the edge, there was no use going any farther. There was no more St. Vith; not one single wall was standing. It looked like a garbage dump with a hilly roadside made in the middle of it. The only building left was the church that we were using. It was unbelievable as we pictured in our minds the beautiful little city that had stood here before.

Relieved from the 82nd Airborne Division on January 23, we were ordered back to our company, which was now at Verviers. As we traveled north, we drove through Malmedy, and as I drove up the hill north of the city, I thought of the narrow escape we had had in getting out of it slightly over a month ago. Now it was back in Belgian hands again; the Germans had been pushed back toward their border once more. After we topped the hill, we were on an open stretch of land, and the traffic was heavy in both directions. Suddenly, we heard the roar of low-flying planes. Looking into my side mirror, I got a glimpse of two fighters roaring off. Lemons said, "I believe they were M-109s." We found out this was true a few minutes later. We had been trained to disperse in case of an enemy air attack. As I drove along, I noticed the oncoming vehicles swerving off the road to their right and into a field. I knew what was coming, and as I swerved off the road to my right and into a field, I heard the rattling roar of machine-gun fire. Ambulance #10 was in front of mine, and a jeep was between us. Before the jeep got off the road, it was hit by machine-gun bullets from one of the ME-109s and exploded. The two men in the jeep were killed. Jones, in #10, swerved but got riddled in the rear. The shells came out through the left side of his ambulance and luckily, just behind the driver's seat. Still, Jones had a close call as the bullets had ripped in close to the gas tank. We jumped from our ambulances and hit the ground. We got a mud bath, as the snow had melted, and the ground was muddy. We thought they would make another pass, but it was a relief to see them speed out of sight.

For a while, we lay in the mud, and no one stirred except the gunners on some trucks and armored half-tracks who were waiting for them if they came back. Then, we rose from the ground and went over to the jeep, which was burning furiously.

The GIs had been blown out of it. Medical officers were already there, but there was nothing they could do for the jeep passengers.

The ground was sloppy, and #10, #11, and other vehicles were stuck in the mud. By this time, other trucks had come up on the scene and a two-and-a-half ton truck winched #11 out and back onto the road. None of the other ambulances were hit, but several had to be winched out also. We arrived at the company quite shaken up and covered with mud, but at least unharmed once again. Upon arriving, though, we learned that our company also had had a narrow escape. A buzz bomb had crashed just a few feet away the night before. Yehle and I walked over to the landing site and looked down into a huge crater about ten feet deep and about twenty feet wide. Nothing was left of the buzz bomb but a few pieces of metal.

Wrecked house and barn near St. Vith

RETURN TO GERMANY

On January 28, our company moved to Brand, Germany, a town southeast of Aachen. The Battle of the Bulge was over; the Germans had made their last futile effort to win the war and failed. Now they were making a frantic attempt to hold back the Allies. Slowly, they retreated toward the Rhine River.

We were resting at Brand. The front was about twenty miles to the east, and it was peaceful and quiet here. We were sharing a number of buildings with an evacuation hospital and several other army units that also were temporarily out of service. One morning, as we returned to our quarters after breakfast, we heard a whistling noise, like a skyrocket. We thought it was shell or bomb, and my ambulance platoon sergeant and I dived under the same cot and collided with each other. We laughed and joked about it after it was over. The noise came from the new jet-propelled plane the Germans had invented, an ME-262 pursuit.

As the First Army pushed the Germans back, the Allies were building up an enormous mass of power in the rear. On February 10, the British armies, the First, the Third, the Seventh, and the Ninth Armies all began to advance together. As the First Army smashed through Duren and pushed toward the Rhine River, thousands of Germans were captured along with massive quantities of guns, trucks, tanks, and supplies. Several bridges had been blown up across the Rhine, and they were trapped on the west side of the big river. Our ambulance platoon was ordered to Duren. Our casualties were not too heavy, but we were keeping close in case we were needed in a hurry.

Another destroyed German tank near the Rhine River,
February 1945

The German armies were trying to flee across the Rhine on the few bridges they had left. They were going to make a stand on the east bank of the Rhine, using it as a natural defense the wideness of the river. They figured that they could destroy any engineer outfit that would try to build a pontoon bridge across the river or kill any troops attempting to cross by boat. The Rhine River was quite wide, and any attempt to get across would prove costly to us. Still, sooner or later, it would have to be done. Duren was completely deserted, and it seemed as though we were the only Americans there. We slept in our ambulances with our doors locked, however, because we were in enemy territory. There was also no place livable but a few lower rooms in some of the buildings, the remaining walls seemed to be ready to fall at any time. There was always the danger of hidden booby traps that had been missed. The Germans had stored most of their valuables in cellars, and china and silverware were still intact and in good shape in many of the closets of the lower rooms and cellars. In addition to the silverware and china, there were a few pieces of furniture here and there unharmed. We left it all undisturbed, as we were trying to respect even the German civilians' personal property. In one of the wrecked homes, which had a couple of walls left and part of the upper floor, was a piano still sitting in its original place and in excellent condition. One of the men climbed up on the rubble, sat down on the stool, and played a tune on it.

At the same time the First Army reached Cologne, Germany, and took the city, the Ninth Army reached the Rhine River across from Dusseldorf on February 12. Cologne was also on the Rhine, and when the armies got to the river, in front of them was a big stream with no bridges to cross over. The Third and Seventh Armies were smashing eastward to the south of us, but the Rhine extended to the southeast, and they had a lot farther to go to reach the river than we did in the north. However, at the speed they were moving, it wouldn't be long before they, too, would be facing the next great obstacle and probably the last before we got to Berlin. Our ambulance platoon moved to Burgheim. Across from where we were parked were the twisted rails of part of a railroad track that had been bombed. Down in a crater in the middle of where the track had been laid was a locomotive resting on its side. One of our bombers had dropped a blockbuster in front of the freight train as it was carrying supplies toward the front earlier in the year or sometime in the past. This town was eight miles from Cologne, and from here, we had to make several trips up to first-aid station to collect some casualties. At one time, we were just a few blocks from the Rhine but close enough to take a picture of the famous Cologne Cathedral, which was close to the river's edge. However, we weren't that anxious to get a look at the Rhine because the enemy was just across on the other side.

Street in Cologne with Cathedral in background. Germans were on the other bank of the river when we took this picture.

THE MIRACULOUS CROSSING OF THE RHINE RIVER

The Ninth and First Armies spread out and secured the west bank of the Rhine River, and then the First Army pushed southward. The plan was to secure a wide stretch along this side as soon as possible so that all of our armies would be facing the Germans across the river side by side. The wider the stretch, the thinner the German line would have to be and the more territory they would have to watch. We would then build up our supplies, build up our units to full strength, and then undertake the crossing about two months later, probably in April. Along this wide stretch, the Germans would not know where the landing on the east bank would be, so it was impossible to concentrate a number of troops in one area. They would have to spread them evenly along the entire stretch.

Our First Army pushed southward toward Bonn, another city on the river. It was taken, and the Ninth Armored Division task forces pushed farther south toward a city called Remagen. The Germans were still trying to get as many troops and equipment across the Rhine as they possibly could on bridges that were still intact. Such was the case of the Ludendorf railroad bridge at Remagen. The Germans were moving train after train across until the last moment possible before blowing it up. When task forces of the Ninth Armored reached Remagen, to their surprise the bridge was still standing. They waited for a while and watched. The bridge remained intact. The general of the Ninth Armored studied the situation. Here was a bridge still standing but loaded with demolitions and ready to be blown up. How many American lives would be lost if a mass of GIs were on the bridge when they blew it up? Still, the bridge remained, and he thought of how many lives would be lost if we had to cross some other way. The general decided to try to take the bridge, as he thought of the great advantage we would have if we could get across and take the bridge intact. Slowly, demolition men climbed along the steel beams and cut one wire after another until they had every charge disconnected. Then the infantrymen of the Ninth Armored started to inch forward on the bridge. The men would hide behind the steel pillars, run about twenty feet, and then hide behind another. Several men were shot before the Americans reached the end of the bridge. A major part of the task was over, but in front of them was a small tunnel that they considered would be a problem. They expected resistance from machine-gun fire but knew the tunnel had to be taken. They stormed the tunnel, and, to their surprise, came upon a bunch of drunken Germans who were having a party.

It was a miracle and something hard to believe for the men of the Ninth Armored. They were on the other side of the Rhine River with very few casualties. Immediately, thousands of infantrymen poured across the bridge to secure the area as quickly as possible. Before they met resistance, they had spread out and established a seven-mile-wide and five-mile-deep beachhead along the east bank of the river. The engineers quickly went to work removing the rails and the ties from the bridge and built a heavy solid-wood floor where the tracks had been. Tanks, half tracks, and field artillery poured across the structure, and we had a solid hold on the east side.

By this time, Berlin got word that a crossing had been made. Soon German bombers appeared in a desperate attempt to knock out the bridge. Artillery units were sending in shells trying to make hits on the bridge.

In the meantime, our ambulance platoon was called from Burgheim. Casualties were increasing as the Germans began to put up a stiff resistance. We drove south to Bad Neuhmar where we ran into danger. It was now dark, and suddenly we began to get fired upon by snipers who were shooting at anyone who came along. They had already killed several GIs. Soon we got some help, and after an hour or so, when they felt it was safe, they let us continue. We drove through the town safely and then were on our way to Remagen.

It took some time to get to this city, as we were driving in the darkness and could barely see the road. We finally arrived and drove through Remagen and came up to the entrance of the Ludendorf Bridge. Our headlights were out and all we had on the front were the tiny pair of cat's-eye lights and pair of very dim taillights in the rear. Both were just bright enough for a close vehicle to see. Except for a jeep that was leading us, #11 was the first ambulance in the convoy. When we reached the entrance, a guard ordered us to halt and asked for the password. After our sergeant gave it to him, the guard warned him that the bridge had been hit by a bomb just a short time before and there was a hole about two-and-a-half feet in the middle of it. He said we could cross, but we would have to be guided by someone. It was one of the darkest nights we had seen, but one of our section leaders, Sergeant Jack Pierce, walked ahead of us holding a white handkerchief. I was the first one to cross, and the rest began to follow. I followed the handkerchief as we slowly traveled across. When we got to the hole, the sergeant checked my front wheels to see that neither one was too close to the edge. I drove over the hole with room to spare for both wheels, and soon began to travel through the tunnel. As each ambulance behind me came to the hole, each one was checked. While we were crossing, several shells splashed into the water, and a few exploded on both sides of the river. The Germans were trying to hit the bridge but couldn't seem to zero in on it. After we all got through the tunnel, our jeep came up ahead again and led us to the 78th Infantry Division clearing station, which was a short distance north of the bridge. After a cup of coffee in the receiving tent, we spread our litters in our ambulance and slept for the rest of the night.

The next morning, after breakfast at the station, Lemons and I had to make a trip across the bridge with a load of casualties and back to an evacuation hospital. By this time, they had mended the hole with a large piece of heavy sheet metal. They had also reinforced the floor with wooden runways about two feet wide and far enough apart for our wheels to travel over. Along with the daylight, it was no trouble to get over the bridge except having to wait for a number of tanks to cross over from the west.

The engineers were working feverishly to get some pontoon bridges built across the river as soon as possible, as the steel structure was the only source we had of crossing. Several times that day, we had to pass over the bridge. The last trip was over to the east side, and it was now nightfall. I could see in the dark fairly well, and both left and right runways were visible. Just as Lemons and I got about halfway across, we heard the roar of a low-flying plane. A German bomber was trying to drop a few bombs on the bridge. Just after it passed overhead, we heard a huge splash in the water about twenty or thirty feet from the bridge. Just a little closer and Lemons, #11, and I would have been "no more." Lemons said, "Whew, that was close."

I said, "Yeah, too close for comfort."

By March 3, the engineers had two pontoon bridges laid across the river in different locations along the stretch we controlled. We stopped using the bridge and the engineers began to work on it. Some heavy equipment had been moved across it, but they didn't trust it, as it appeared to be weak. The engineers decided that before any more traffic crossed over, it would have to be reinforced. It was impossible to bring heavy equipment over on the pontoon bridges. Ambulances, tanks, and trucks were okay, but for the heavier equipment, larger pontoons would have to be brought in.

Several 240 mm guns on long trailers had been brought across and were parked on the east side. The barrels were probably twice as long as the gun barrels on the battleships behind us on the Normandy coast. At least, they looked that much longer. They were also much louder, and several times, they fired as I passed them. The blast of the guns stung my eardrums. For several days, it affected my hearing, so we put cotton in our ears when we came close to them to help stifle the noise. This seemed to help some. The guns proved to be effective, as they had a long range. It was bad for the railroad bridge, however, which vibrated every time a shell was fired.

COLLAPSE OF THE LUDENDORF BRIDGE

It was on March 7 when the catastrophe occurred. Lemons and I were summoned to carry a load of wounded Germans from the 78th Infantry Division clearing station to a German military hospital at Ling on the east side of the Rhine a few miles south of the bridge. On our return trip, I decided to take a picture of the railroad bridge so I could show friends and relatives the bridge we crossed in the miraculous crossing of the Rhine River. I stopped about a half mile south of the bridge, took out my trusty little Kodak, and snapped a picture of the famous Ludendorf Railroad Bridge, which would make worldwide history in just a few moments. Satisfied, I jumped back into #11, and we headed north toward the bridge. Each time we made a trip, we would look up at the steel structure to see what progress was being made, assuming that someday we would be traveling over it once again. This time, a huge crane was moving on the west wing toward the middle span. To get past the bridge, we had to drive under the east wing. It was a dusty road we were traveling on, and dust rose behind our ambulance. As we approached the wing, we slowed down, and the dust settled.

The 240 mm guns were still in use, and we were expecting to hear one of them fire away. Suddenly, as we were directly under the east wing, we heard a loud cracking noise, then several more. Lemons and I jumped in our seats and almost hit the ceiling of #11. I suspected some steel beams were snapping, so I floored the accelerator. Just as we cleared the bridge, one end of the east wing dropped on the road, right on the spot we had been a second before. Immediately, we were hidden in a cloud of dust. When we cleared the dust cloud, we heard a tremendous splash out in the river. When we looked toward the water, most of the bridge had gone under except for some twisted metal sticking out of the water in several places. The vehicle with the crane had disappeared, and several boats were speeding to the wreckage, possibly to pick up any survivors who might have escaped from the wreckage or the crane and were swimming around. We heard later that there were several casualties or fatalities. The near hits by the German bombers and the concussion from the 240s, along with the heavy equipment on it, proved too much for the bridge and weakened it until it snapped and collapsed. Some of the wooden beams that had made up the floor had snapped, and jagged pieces began to float along the river, bursting several air-filled pontoons and knocking out one of the pontoon bridges temporarily until the pontoons could be replaced with new ones. However, this wasn't too serious, as now there were a number of floating bridges built across the river that were in use.

We stopped just a short distance from the scene, and when I recovered from the scare, I took another snapshot, this time of the wreckage resting in the water. When I climbed back into the ambulance, I said to Lemons, "Well, that's another close one we had."

Lemons said, "Yeah, we've been having too many of those lately." Jokingly, he added, "Are you caught up on your prayers?" Truthfully, I couldn't have answered a yes on that. About the only time I prayed was when I got in danger. The bridge incident happened so quickly we didn't have time — just time enough to get ourselves and #11 out of the way.

We moved north with the 78th Medical Clearing Station on March 10 to Konegsiventer. We were still close to the river, and while we were waiting for the kitchen to set up, we looked around in some of the buildings nearby. In one of them were several large wine vats, one of them having a hole in the top of it. When we looked into it, we saw a dead German floating on top of the remaining wine. We placed a sign in front of the vat to let everyone know what was in there. As we came out of the winery, we heard the whistle of a jet plane again. Once more, we could see the jet banking one way and then the other, but the German pilot didn't have too much to worry about, as they were still firing behind him. It was a reconnaissance plane, probably taking pictures of the collapsed bridge.

We were still evacuating across the river to the evacuation hospitals. The traffic eastward was heavy, as tanks, supply trucks, and all sorts of vehicles were pouring across the floating rubber bridges. There was not enough room for an airstrip yet, and they had not yet captured any airfields on this side of the river. Therefore, we still had to rely on the pontoon bridges, and they were being used to the utmost. Coming back from one of these trips, we came under another air attack. Several bombers came over and dropped their bombs. Just before it happened, one of the other ambulances had been in front, and we had been keeping a 100-yard interval, which we were required to do as we approached the pontoon bridge. A large 2 1/2-ton truck passed and got in front of me, so I had to slow down to widen the interval again. We were about a mile from the river when the attack came, and a bomb landed in the road in front of the truck ahead of us.

The 2 1/2-ton truck veered off the road and turned over. The driver was killed, and the assistant driver was wounded.

We gave him the best first-aid treatment we could, and then they rushed the black soldier off in a jeep. Several pieces of the truck hit #11, but the only damage was a little paint scraped off. I thought afterwards that the driver of the truck had unknowingly sealed his own destiny and saved our lives by pulling in front of us and causing me to slow down.

The Germans did not have time enough to reorganize fully on this side of the Rhine, and we were now beginning to expand and advance. The Third Armored Division task forces were again spearheading, and the infantry divisions were securing the left and right flanks of the paths on which they traveled. We were beginning to have good weather now. It was getting warmer, the snow had melted, the ground was drying up, and there was no more worry of our vehicles getting stuck in the mud.

On March 25, we traveled with the 78th Infantry Division Medical Clearing Station to Hackenburg, sixty miles east of the Rhine. An airfield had been captured, and we were evacuating back to the 5th and 44th Evacuation Hospitals, which set up their tents and equipment beside the airstrip. The Ruhr area around the Rhine River was now completely encircled, the infantry divisions were mopping up the weak resistance, and a wide section of the east bank was secured. A multitude of large pontoon bridges had been assembled across the river, several airstrips had been taken, and the Germans were losing ground. We were again pushing forward, and the future seemed to be in our favor.

The 78th Infantry Medical Clearing Station moved to Wurgendorf, Germany, on April 1. We were now transporting wounded over a distance of sixty miles one way, but on April 3, we moved on up to a Third Armored 45th Medical first-aid station, which was with one of the task forces. We started eastward with the task force of the Third Armored from an area south of Paderborn. All the Allied armies from north to south were pushing forward, as the Germans were concentrating most of their remaining power on the eastern front, trying to hold back the Russians. They feared the Reds more than they did the Allies. It was assumed by the Germans that if Russia took over Germany, the Germans would be slaves for years and years, whereas if the Allies took over most of their territory, they could look forward to being free again sometime in the near future.

Several days passed by, and we had advanced about fifty miles eastward. We still had to proceed with caution, as the men in the front of the column never knew when a German 88 mm was pointed at them from around a curve or at a crossroad behind a building. I was driving #11 not too far from the front vehicle. A jeep, several tanks, and a few trucks were in front of me. I was only about a half mile or less behind the leading vehicle. Several times, we had to stop because of sniper fire, and we had to wait until they killed or captured the snipers. We started to move again, and suddenly a big battle broke loose up ahead. Stopping once again and inquiring about what was going on, we found that fifteen enemy tanks had attacked the front of the column. We had pulled over to the shoulder of the road and were waiting. Instantly, from the woods on both sides of us, a number of German tanks came crashing through and out into the pastures and commenced firing at the tanks in front and back of #11. Lemons and I figured this was it for us, but once again we were spared as a number of P-47 Thunderbolts appeared and began dive-bombing. It wasn't too long before the enemy tanks were a mass of wreckage and burning fiercely. We were glad to see our Thunderbolts, but this was just about the hottest battle Lemons and I had experienced. This was one time that even our own planes were too close for comfort. While the P-47s were knocking out the last tank that had attacked us here, other Thunderbolts went to work on the fifteen tanks up ahead. Soon, they, too, were wiped out, and we began to move on. Two of our Sherman tanks were destroyed and the tank men killed.

Since the ground was quite dry now, the task force commander decided to start traveling across country through fields and farms to stay off the roads and confuse the Germans, come up behind them, and capture them or wipe them out. This seemed to work, and more than once our tanks sneaked up behind some of the enemy's tanks and guns, capturing or destroying them. We bivouacked at night, setting up only the kitchen tent. The nights were fair and clear, the men slept on the ground, we slept in our ambulance, and the next day we started again through more pastures and fields. None of them had been plowed yet, as the farmers had fled or were serving in the German army.

On April 12, we passed through the city of Nordhausen, which was also in ruins. The streets had to be cleared. Some of them were impassable because of the wreckage from the buildings. They put German POWs to work on this to make it easier for other divisions to follow.

Leaving Nordhausen behind, we pushed toward the burg of Sangerhausen. As we neared the village, we were attacked by a flight of Focke-Wulfes that strafed the column. As one of the Germans came down for another pass, his plane was struck by antiaircraft fire. The plane belly-landed in a field about a quarter of a mile from us. A number of infantrymen ran over to perhaps pull him out if they could, but it was too late. The plane exploded and was burning so fiercely they couldn't get to him.

We received the news on April 13 through the Signal Corps that President Franklin D. Roosevelt had died suddenly. This placed the top job in the hands of Vice President Harry S Truman of Independence, Missouri. Lemons and I left the same morning for the rear with a load of patients.

THE NORDHAUSEN CONCENTRATION CAMP

We had to evacuate our patients back to Nordhausen where an evacuation hospital had been set up. When we arrived at the hospital, we found that it had been set up next to a concentration camp where the Germans had inhumanely treated thousands of Poles, Jews, Russians, and people of other nationalities. We walked over to the camp, and as we stepped inside the gate, we held a sight that will never be forgotten.

Lying side by side on the ground in three rows from one end of the camp to the other were bodies of human beings, some of them with arms and legs missing. All of the bodies were decomposed and looked like skeletons. We had heard that there were several hundred survivors rescued from the dead. The survivors were placed in army hospitals. We also heard about the horrible atrocities that had been committed here by the Germans. It was rumored that they cut tattoos off some of these people and made lampshades out of the tattoos. However, seeing the dead lying here was enough evidence to prove that they had been horribly treated. We walked along by the side of the buildings, and through an open door in one of them, we saw a gas chamber where the Nazis had herded them in like cattle and killed a roomful at a time. The stench of the dead was nauseating, so Lemons and I hurried out of the area and back to the hospital. We stepped into the receiving tent and saw some of the survivors. The tent was just about full of them, and they all looked like living skeletons.

Bodies of the inmates who were imprisoned at the Nordhausen Concentration Camp, April 1945

Lemons and I left in #11 and returned to Company C of the Third Armored 45th Medical Battalion but found that the treatment station had left and moved on with the task force to Belleben. Since the infantry had not yet come up to secure the areas on both sides of the road, we were alone with a possible enemy to the left and right of us, so with tenseness, we drove #11 along, hoping we wouldn't be fired upon. When we came in sight of the Sherman tanks, we were relieved. However, they were firing away, and we had to proceed with caution until we found the treatment station. The medical captain told us that the task force had met some more resistance. The tanks finally crashed into Belleben and the first-aid station set up in a tavern for the night. We slept upstairs on the floor on our blankets for the night but were awakened occasionally by the fire from the tanks and by incoming enemy shell fire.

111

The next morning, April 14, Lemons and I had to carry dead GIs to a graves registration station. We turned their belongings over to the officers in command, then carried the dead men out and laid them on the ground on the stretchers. Lying on a stretcher next to them were the remains of a sergeant whose entire body was blasted away. Nothing was left but his head, his legs, and a strip of skin joining them. We walked away shaking our heads, knowing that some loved ones back in the States would soon get the word from the War Department.

As we traveled back to the treatment station, we came up to a woman who was standing in the road waving a pistol. We wondered what was about to take place, as we never knew what to expect, considering all that we had encountered. As I came by the side of her, she shoved the pistol to me as she talked away in German. We assumed that someone had told her to turn all weapons in, and she thought she was supposed to turn them in to the Americans. However, what she was supposed to have done was to turn them in to the burgomaster's (mayor's) office with her name on a tag tied to the gun for registration so she could get it back in the future.

Just a little after noon, our task force moved on. Several of our ambulances were together, and a few miles east of Belleben, we ran into sniper fire. A bullet smashed into the side window of one of the ambulances, barely missing the driver and assistant. Another ambulance was hit. The red crosses didn't seem to make any difference. In fact, it appeared as if the Germans were using them for target practice instead of bull's-eyes. Once again, we split up, each ambulance placed behind a tank carrying a dozen or more infantrymen. When the snipers would fire, the men would jump off the tank, search out the sniper, and kill him.

We made our way through the town of Konnern, and the column stopped after pushing forward for a mile. The tanks ahead of us ran into resistance, and the entire column was proceeding cautiously to protect as many GIs as possible. I had a pair of binoculars and used them quite often. Through them, I saw action sometimes that I otherwise would not have seen. The terrain was quite level in this area, and as I stood on the road looking across several fields, I noticed some German trucks speeding along another road. At the same moment, two jeeps loaded with infantrymen came down our road, turned into a side road in front of us, and headed in that direction. The trucks drove out of sight, but in a few minutes, we heard gunfire, and we assumed that the infantrymen had caught up with them.

Just before we started to move again, a colonel came along with his driver and with two civilians sitting on the hood of their jeep. The jeep turned off onto a dirt road and drove into a patch of woods nearby. We heard several shots, and then the colonel and his driver came out of the woods without the civilians. We learned later that they were not civilians but German soldiers who had killed seven men.

After driving about a quarter of a mile, another jeep came down the road with a German soldier. Since #11 was the first ambulance in the column, the driver stopped, and the medical officer of Company C, 45th medics, told me to carry him back to a civilian hospital in Konnern. Upon arriving at Konnern, I came up to the scene of an accident. An MP belonging to another task force was lying on the ground. He had been crushed between two trucks and was in pain. An MP lieutenant took the

German out of #11 and put him in a POW lineup of about fifty Germans. He then ordered me to take the injured MP to the Third Armored first-aid station of his task force, which was Company A. We were on our own now and had to search for Company A, but with the assistance of the MP, we found the first-aid station. Now we had to find our way back. We had turned on several different roads. One road looked like another, and when we came to one crossroad, we turned left. We drove along and came to a small town. Here the civilians ran into their houses. About a mile or two farther, we came to another town. It was strange to us, and we knew then that we were on the wrong road, in enemy territory between the two task forces. Just as we started to turn around, a German officer walked out from the town and up to the ambulance. Lemons was driving, so I stepped out of #11 to meet him. We saluted each other, and he spoke English well enough to ask me if I had come to take over the town, that he was ready to turn it over to me. I told him that the infantry would be in later and when he saw them coming to wave a white flag. I saluted him again and climbed back into #11. We turned around and started back in the direction we had come from when suddenly, from one of the buildings, a shot was fired. The bullet hit the ambulance in the side somewhere and bounced off. I said to Lemons, "Let's get out of here." We sped away and figured it would be best to go back through the first town we had come through where the civilians had run into the houses and then to the road where we had turned off wrong in the first place.

We came to the town and there were no civilians in sight, but as we drove around a curve in the road, we came face to face with a German tank in the middle of the road. Lemons and I didn't know what would happen next but were hoping the tank men would observe the red crosses on the front of ambulance

#11. We approached them slowly, with tenseness. Lemons was still driving, and as we approached the tank, the Germans were eyeing us, and we were eyeing them. They let us pass unharmed, and we were relieved, realizing they had respected our red crosses. They didn't try to stop us or take us prisoner, as they, too, realized the end of the war wasn't too far off.

When we arrived at the crossroad where we had turned off wrong, we met one of the task forces. I told the commander about the German officer and about the sniper and then about the tankers letting us pass. The commander assured me that if they would surrender without fighting, he would let the tank men live. He also thanked me for warning him about the sniper, saying he would approach the second town with caution. I drew a map showing the location of the building where the shot had come from.

We finally found our way back to the Third Armored treatment station of Company C and continued with them. When darkness approached, we pulled into a field where Lemons and I slept in our ambulance for the night. When the next morning came, we were ordered to carry a load of wounded back to the 98th Evacuation Hospital, a 100-mile trip to the rear. We left the first-aid station and headed back toward Konnern. Just before we reached the town, I noticed through some cracks in a barn that we passed, several German vehicles. One of the cracks was wide enough for me to recognize that one of them was a German half-track. I checked the mileage to Konnern, and upon arriving, I told a tank driver and gave him the exact mileage to the barn. The Germans may have been hiding and intending to give trouble later on, or they may have been intending to give themselves up later on. Many of the Germans were beginning to surrender themselves, but it was always possible to run into a bunch of diehards who might show some resistance.

We continued on our way, and when we arrived at the hospital, we found out that we were relieved. However, we had to remain at the hospital until our company was located. It was now April 15. The weather was pleasant, and in the afternoon, we left the hospital and carried a load of combat-exhaustion patients back to a combat-exhaustion center. This was a 286-mile round trip, one of the longest trips we had made, but somehow it didn't seem as tiresome as some of those we had to make while we were spearheading with the task forces. There were times when we were on the move for three consecutive days with the Third Armored unites and barely had time to take turns in catnapping, as we carried patients back from the front and returned. This was the only trip we made at the hospital, however, and we were getting a much-needed rest.

Across from the evacuation hospital was a heavily wooded area. On the morning of April 22, Yehle's assistant drive, Roy Deem, and I were strolling around in the woods. We found a number of German Mauser rifles and cartridges. We loaded up the rifles and decided to go deer hunting, as we had seen a few deer earlier. After walking around for a while, we came back to where we found the rifles and ammunition and started to shoot at the trees. We found out that these were powerful rifles. The bullets would rip through the center of a tree eight inches in diameter. We had just laid the guns down when we noticed a group of German soldiers coming in our direction, along a gravel road where we were standing.

They were fully equipped, guns and all, and had already seen us. We had our red cross armbands on and I said to

Folke Wolf 190 in perfect condition at a German Luftwaffe
Base at Halle, Germany, April 1945

Deem, "There's no use of us moving away like we are afraid of
them." So, we held our ground. We were sitting on a dirt bank
on the side of the road as they passed by us. We flipped our
hands up and said, "Hi!" to them. They grinned, said something
in German, and went on. There seemed to be a mutual feeling
with each other that the war was almost over, anyway, so why
kill each other? The Allied forces were close to Berlin. In fact,
the Russians already surrounded the city. This little group of
Germans was probably trying to sneak home to their families.

On April 25, our ambulance platoon joined up with the
rest of our company at a German airfield at Halle, Germany.
Here we saw a number of German bombers with fighter planes
mounted on top of them. They were called "piggy back" planes.
The fighters could not carry enough fuel to reach London,

One of the many planes that were smashed by an Allied bombing raid at Halle, Germany, April 1945

Some of these planes were still smoldering when we arrived at this airfield in Halle

Destroyed by Germans before retreating

England, and return, so the bombers would carry them on top until they got to London. Then they would disengage them and the fighters could protect them on the bombing run and still have enough fuel left to return to German territory.

The same day we arrived at the Halle airbase, the American forces joined the Russians at Torgau. Our work was about to cease, as very few casualties were coming in. most of the German army had been captured, and what was left was surrendering to the Allies, with no resistance. The only area holding out was Berlin where they were bitterly resisting the Russians. The Allied forces in Italy were rushing up toward Switzerland and France.

On May 1, the entire company moved to Naumberg, south of Halle, and into a large building about a mile from the business district. Hitler had caused his own German people a great discomfort. Food for them was scarce. It was difficult for us to see them scrape out of the garbage cans the scraps that we had thrown away. I had heard that during the Depression of 1929 some of our people were so hungry that they would pick up food from the streets, but I never experienced anything like that. My father had a job and kept on working, and we at least had good, clean food to eat. But here we were seeing hungry people eating from the cans. The cooks would give them what was left over in the pots, but there was never enough to feed all who came around.

It was on May 4 that we heard some news. Word was out that Hitler had committed suicide in an underground bomb shelter under the chancellery in Berlin. Other rumors spread around that he wasn't dead at all and that he had the dead story spread around. Later, they claimed that they had identified his teeth from dental work he had done, so it was assumed that he was dead. Nevertheless, a new leader took his place — Admiral Doenitz.

German hotel at Naumberg, Germany, where we stayed until we were ready to return to the States, May 1945

Looking down from the hotel at the city of Naumber into the
valley below, June 1945

On May 7, Admiral Doenitz notified all of the German forces to
lay down their arms and announced the surrender of his forces
to the Allies.

May 8, President Truman, the Prime Minister of England,
Premier Stalin of Russia, and the other heads of state of the
Allies officially announced the cessation of all hostilities in
Europe. The war was definitely over in this area. We listened on
the radio to hundreds of whistles blowing in London. The
people in Paris went wild, but New York celebrated
conservatively because we were still at war with Japan.

The next day, after the war was over, however, we
experienced a few tense moments when an ME-109 German
fighter swooped down on the building where we were staying.
Since we had been under strafings by these planes not too long
before, we were still "battle conscious" even though the war had

ended. We thought a German pilot might have hidden somewhere and sneaked out to get a plane with the idea of staging a one-man war against us. It was very quickly spread, though, that a U.S. fighter pilot had taken one of our medical officers up for a flight in his plane, which was in perfect condition and unharmed.

We thought our work was finished, but on June 7 our ambulance platoon was sent on detached service to Merseburg, Germany. We were given the job of transporting displaced persons back to their border. Hitler had taken these Russians from their homes and had herded them like cattle in boxcars to Germany, forcing them to work in factories. We loaded up #11 with a group of Russian civilians and carried them to Torgau on the Russian side of the lines. As we crossed over into the Russian lines and looked at the Russians, not many of them smiled or waved. We got a cool reception, and it almost felt as if we were in hostile territory once again. Occasionally, a Russian soldier would wave, but most of them seemed to have an unfriendly attitude. There were women soldiers, hard looking, and battle worn. They had belts of machine gun bullets crisscrossed in front and strapped on them from their waists to their shoulders. We turned the civilians over to the Russian authorities and returned to our side. We were then relieved and we returned to the company.

On June 16, I was ordered to drive a medical officer in #11 to Paris. During combat, we had been traveling over fields and two-lane roads, but now we were able to try out the four-lane superhighways the Germans had built for military purposes and for civilian use later on. I had never seen any four-lane highways back home. I don't believe we had any yet, and it seemed nice driving along, separated from the oncoming traffic.

122

The superhighways were built outside of the towns, and it was possible to go for miles and miles without stopping unless we came to a bombed-out section of the road. We traveled 400 miles across Germany on one of these "Reich autobahns" to the city of Luxembourg, in the small nation of Luxembourg. During this trip, we passed by a number of beautiful modern homes unlike anything we had in the United States. They looked like something in the future, even though the Germans already had them built and were living in them.

We left Luxembourg at 7:30 a.m. on June 17 and stopped for a while at Verdun, France. We saw the monument erected there for the soldiers who had fought and died in World War I. In one area, French bayonets were sticking straight up out of the ground. This place was roped off, and a marker was there that told what had happened. A number of French soldiers had been buried alive by a German artillery assault, the shells exploding nearby and huge masses of dirt covering them up before they could escape. The bayonets were still held by the skeletons of the men who had been buried alive. On the floor of the monument, which was a building, and along the front of it were compartments enclosed by windows. Each compartment was filled with skulls and bones of soldiers who had died during the battle of Verdun. We went inside the monument to look around. On the walls of the rooms were hundred of pictures showing buildings that were in the area in 1917 and drawings portraying battles that were fought during the First World War. At the front of the monument, on the outside, was a huge plaque, and engraved on it were thousands of names of the soldiers who participated in the battles.

We left Verdun and reached Paris after driving seventy miles. We had rooms reserved for us at a hotel, and meals were available at the motor pool where I parked #11. When the captain went somewhere, he would tell me the approximate time he would be back, and I was free during the time he was gone. I had the entire afternoon to myself one day, so I walked to the Eiffel Tower, which wasn't too far away. An elevator carried me up to the first level, and then I had to climb quite a few steps to the second level. That was as far as anyone could go, as the U.S. Air Force was still using the observation tower at the top as an observation post. But even the second level was very high, and I was able to see all over Paris. It was a magnificent sight, and I concluded that it was one of the most beautiful cities in the world. Comparing it to Washington, D.C., it was hard to decide which was the prettiest, except for the fact that the United States was my country, so I picked Washington.

I came down and stood by the tower, looking up at it, amazed at its tremendous size. Suddenly, a P-38 Lockheed twin-fuselage fighter swooped down from the sky and made a pass under the arch of the tower. Then, moments later, a P-51 Mustang swooped down and zoomed through the arch. I thought to myself, *those crazy nuts*. I guess they figured that since they made it through the war alive, they would try to accomplish a daredevil stunt so they could say when they got home that they flew under the arch of the Eiffel Tower.

After enjoying three days in Paris, we left on June 20 and traveled to Compeigne, then Soissons, and then on to Reims. We stayed at Reims overnight and left in the morning. On the way north, we passed more World War I trenches at a small town called Vouziers and arrived at Huy, Belgium, that evening. The captain had become acquainted with a sugar company executive during our stay there while the Battle of the Bulge was taking place. He was invited back, and while we were

Napoleon's Tomb, June 1945

125

The Eiffel Tower, June, 1945

there, I, too, was treated like royalty. I was assigned to a large guest room with a wonderful bed and a private bathroom. Once again, I felt like a king. We stayed at Huy for several days, and then returned to Naumberg on June 24.

Upon our return, we heard rumors that we were going to be shipped to the Far East, but we also heard other rumors that a number of us were going to be discharged on a point system. It would be figured on a marital basis and the amount of time each man had served in the army. Since I was married and had been in the service for four years, I had accumulated eighty-eight points. Most of the other ambulance drivers had enough points to be eligible as well.

On July 1, our entire ambulance platoon left the company and was attached to the 175th Medical Battalion at Marburg. We welcomed this change, as it was beginning to get boring at Naumberg. We didn't have much to do and spent a lot of time doing it. Here it wasn't much different except that we did have a change of scenery. Occasionally, they used one of our ambulances to carry a load of enlisted men who became sick back to a station hospital in Geissen.

It was on one of these trips that I had a new kind of experience. It was the first time that I had ever killed anything in my life. I had just left a first-aid station in Marburg and had driven out into open country when I came up to three geese in the middle of the road. I slowed down, blew my horn, and drove slowly forward. Two of the geese moved out of the road, but one of them stood there honking. It was a gander and much bigger than the other two. He was acting stubborn about it, but I figured when I got close enough he would finally move. I kept moving until I couldn't see him any longer over the front of the ambulance. I said to Lemons, "I wonder if he moved." Just then, we heard a "CRUNCH," and I knew I had run over a stubborn goose. As we drove away from the spot, a German woman ran out of her house and grabbed the goose, carrying it to her home. The geese probably belonged to her, and she probably had goose for supper that evening.

We sweated it out for a month at Marburg, halfway expecting to be shipped out and transported toward Japan but hoping, at the same time, that something would happen to change our destiny. Sure enough, it did.

ATOMIC BOMB DROP AND THE SURRENDER OF JAPAN

The astounding news came to us over the radio on August 7. President Truman gave the order to drop a new type of bomb on Japan — an atomic bomb. This type of bomb had been dropped on an undisclosed area and tested. It had covered an immense area with destruction and was estimated to have the capability of destroying an entire city. On the morning of August 7, an atomic bomb was dropped on Hiroshima, a city in Japan. The destruction it caused shocked the world. The next day, another atomic bomb was dropped on the city of Nagasaki. Again, the entire city was destroyed. On August 9, Russia declared war on Japan. Dropping these bombs seemed inhumane, but in reality, it saved an enormous amount of lives because it was uncertain how long the war would last and how many lives would be lost during that time.

The Japanese realized it was useless to continue fighting any longer since they faced the threat of having more cities destroyed by these bombs. On August 10, they offered to surrender unconditionally providing Emperor Hirohito remained as leader of their country. The United States, England, and Russia communicated with each other and sent back their reply on August 11. Hostilities ceased, and on August 14, a formal surrender was made on a battleship just outside of the Tokyo harbor.

We were still attached to the 175th Medical Battalion but felt sure now that we wouldn't be shipped to the Far East and that in a short time, we would be on our way home. We knew that there would be an army of occupation but with the number of points we had built up, we figured we would not have to participate in that.

Twelve days passed by and then, on the twenty-sixth of August, I was transferred from the 175th Medical Battalion to Company, 12th Armored Ordinance Battalion of the 5th Armored Division. Grant Trader, who drove #7, was transferred with me. As we left, we said farewell to Yehle, Lemons, and several of the other ambulance drivers. We drove ambulance #7 and ambulance #11 to Allendorf and parked them in the motor pool of the ordinance battalion. We knew now that we were on the way home, and moments began to seem like hours, hours like days, and days like months during the week we spent there.

On September 1, the order came for us to leave. Grant and I climbed into the back of a 2 1/2-ton truck with a group of men, and we started on our journey. As we left, we passed right by #7 and #11, and we looked at them until we got out of sight. It was just like saying good-bye to some old friends. They had served us well all the way through combat, and now we were parting.

We traveled for quite a while, stopping occasionally for a break. Finally, in the evening, we pulled into a bivouac area at Kaiserlautern, Germany, where we stayed overnight. We still had all of our equipment, and it was sort of hard to handle, as most of us had one or two souvenirs. I had a Nazi flag and a German helmet with me, the flag not being any trouble, but the helmet was bulky in my duffle bag. However, we didn't have to carry them too far. We left Kaiserlautern the next morning and rolled into another bivouac area at Nancy, France, in the afternoon.

Next morning, we left Nancy and traveled to Camp Atlanta. I cannot remember where it was situated. We stayed there for eleven days, from September 3 to the 13. We were getting anxious now because we were traveling toward home, and the time seemed to be dragging by for Grant and me. Finally, on September 13, we boarded a train and arrived at Camp Twenty Grand, an embarkation point for troops going back to the States. This camp was just a few miles outside the city of Le Havre. We didn't know it at the time, but we had a two-week wait there.

A strange thing happened at this place that Grant and I will always remember. We were not far from a post exchange where we could buy soft drinks, magazines, and candy. They also sold wristwatches and silver bracelets with the Eiffel Tower and the Arc de Triomphe engraved on them and many other things. The silver watches and bracelets were disappearing, and it appeared as if some stealing were going on. The building had not been broken into, but a guard was placed outside during the night. More objects were stolen, and they thought perhaps the stealing was happening during the daytime. A guard was placed on duty during opening hours, but nothing happened. The next morning, some more merchandise had disappeared. We had been warned about the consequences of stealing and the penalties of getting caught, but since it seemed to be disappearing at night, it was a mystery. One night, a guard was placed in the post exchange near the merchandise, just after closing time. Suddenly, he heard a noise, and when he shined his flashlight in the direction of the watches and bracelets, he saw a huge rat with a watch in its mouth. I had heard of pack rats before but had never seen any in action. This pack rat quickly took off and disappeared with the watch. The next morning, a hole was found in the floor of the building, so they began to tear up the floor and found all of the merchandise on the ground.

A bulletin of apology was sent to us throughout the camp by the commander and an announcement of who the real culprit was. The floor was repaired and no further "stealing" occurred.

September 28 came, and we received the order to pack up. We were leaving. Once again, we were filled with excitement and more so when we arrived at the Le Havre harbor. This city was at least 100 miles east and slightly north of the Normandy coast where we had first landed. We walked up the gangplank of the S.S. *Lewiston Victory*, and about an hour later, the victory ship started to move away from the pier. In the harbor ahead of us was a graveyard of all types of ships, just the masts and smokestacks sticking up out of the water. Allied bombers or torpedoes had probably sunk these ships. Our ship had to maneuver between the sunken derelicts as the ship's pilot made his way toward sea. After we passed the last wreck, the harbor pilot got off and left the ship to the captain. Soon land disappeared, and we were in the open sea headed west-southwest toward the States.

It was September 28, and hurricane season was still on. Not too far from the mainland of France, the sea began to get rough and the weather also. The wind was blowing forcefully, and the waves were crashing over the bow of the ship. It could very well have been the remains of a hurricane, or it was a strong channel storm, as we were still in the English Channel.

The food on this American ship was much better than what we had received on the way to England, but, of course, the British probably couldn't help it because they had been at war two years longer than we had been. The coffee was the best I had tasted in over two years. For dinner, we would get a slice of ham as large as a ten-inch plate or a pork chop as large as a t-bone steak, and all we wanted to eat. But the weather, being rough, caused most of us to become seasick, and it ruined our appetites.

The salt air closed the pores of my skin, and I began to get a large painful boil on my jaw under my lower lip on the right side. The trip began to get miserable as we bounced around in the rough Atlantic. One of the rough nights, I had to pull a two-hour shift of guard duty to watch and listen for the blast of an oncoming ship. We had come into an area where the sea was calm, but there was a thick fog. A watch was posted to assist the captain. If I heard a ship's whistle, I was to shine a flashlight up at his pilot room to warn him. Every four minutes, the captain would blow the ship's horn to warn another ship coming in our direction. Every precaution was being taken to avoid a collision since we were in the middle of the shipping lanes. The two hours seemed like ages, as I felt seasick and I was uncomfortable with a swollen jaw. Finally, I was relieved, and I went back to my bunk to lie down. In the morning, the seas began to get wild again and remained like that for several days. On the morning of October 10, however, the sea became calm. It began to get warm, the sun came out, and a cloud was nowhere to be seen. We stood at the front of the ship and, looking down, watched the porpoises racing and playing at the bow. Looking off to the side, I saw a fin sticking out of the water and assumed it was a large shark. We watched the flying fish as they would jump out and glide along above the water. Seagulls began to follow the ship, and we got some bread scraps from the ship's kitchen, threw them up in the air, and watched the birds dive down and catch them in their beaks.

THE GREAT RECEPTION

The entire Fifth Armored Division was on the ship, and although Grant and I were the only representatives of our ambulance platoon, we felt as though we were part of the Fifth. We were told that we were off the coast and not very far from Long Island. Suddenly, someone shouted that the Ambrose Lightship was ahead. In just a few moments, the rails were crowded with men on all the decks. Only someone who had been away from the States and was coming back could realize the joyful feeling we had within us. Several men came out carrying a banner about forty feet long that read *Fifth Armored Division*. They lowered it and draped it on the side of the ship.

We were getting filled with anxiety now, looking ahead to see the skyscrapers loom their tops up above the water. Suddenly, someone shouted, "There's Long Island!" Off in the distance to the right, I could see the shoreline of Fire Island, the narrow strip of land between Long Island and the ocean. We had passed the Ambrose Lightship about 2:30 p.m.; it was about 4:00 p.m. when someone saw the skyscrapers. We all looked forward and watched, as the tops seemed to rise out of the water.

The skyscrapers rose higher, and soon they were in full view. The shoreline of Long Island and Brooklyn was in clear sight when someone spotted the Statue of Liberty. Sure enough, ahead of us was that beautiful lady standing there with her arm in the air and her lamp still burning as she held it up in her hand. As we passed by the side of her, tears of joy were falling from the eyes of many of us who, two years or more before, wondered if we would ever see her again. My jaw was now swollen badly, and it seemed as if I had a golf ball in my mouth, but the joyful sight helped to keep my mind off the pain.

As we approached Manhattan, a number of sirens began to scream on Long Island. I thought at first it might be another fire on the island, but we were told that the fire companies were notified that the Fifth Armored Division was coming in, and they were putting New York City on the alert that we were approaching. All the ships coming toward us now were blowing their whistles. As we swung to the left, we began to enter the Hudson River. Sirens were screaming, boat whistles were blowing, and ticker tape began to stream from the windows of the skyscrapers that were now directly to the right of us. A boat pulled up by the right side of the ship because on this side was where all the action was, and a band started playing. We were getting a hero's welcome and we were soaking it up.

We reached the George Washington Bridge and passed under it. Then things began to quiet down. At 6 p.m., we arrived at the Camp Shanks pier, but it wasn't until 9 p.m. that we left the ship and went in trucks to the barracks that were prepared for us. Here at the barracks, I found my brother waiting. Since he was still in the signal corps, he knew exactly when I would be in and where I would be placed. About 10 p.m. that night, I called home and spoke to my wife, mom, dad, and sister.

The next morning, I went on sick call since I was in a great deal of pain. The doctor gave me a penicillin shot and a bottle of alcohol. He told me that if it didn't get better, he would lance it and put me in the hospital. I didn't like that at all. I didn't mind the lancing part, but I didn't want anything to hinder me from going home, so I bathed my jaw all night long in alcohol. In the morning, the poison broke loose from the outside, and it stopped hurting. I kept bathing the infection and got all the poison out of it, and it began to heal.

On October 8, Grant and I, still with each other, left Camp Shanks, New York, with a trainload of GIs and arrived at Fort Dix, New Jersey. Grant and I had begun our army careers here in 1941 and now we were about to end them together at the same camp.

October 10, we were placed on the roster for discharge and began our processing. We were offered sergeant rating if we would reenlist, but both Grant and I said, "No, we want out."

On October 12, we received our discharges at 11 a.m., and a truck carried us to the railroad station at Trenton, where I said farewell to Grant, as he was headed south to Bridgeton, New Jersey. They gave us travel pay, so I immediately bought my ticket, caught the next train northbound, and soon was on my way to New York. I was going to have to wait until 5 p.m. for a train to Medford and get there about 7 p.m. I decided to take an earlier train to Patchogue, and I arrived there at 3 p.m. they were expecting me on the 7 p.m. train, so I knew I could surprise them. I got into a cab at the railroad station and was soon on the road north to Medford.

When I got to Medford, I told the cab driver to turn off on a side road and out of sight of the house, as they could look down the main road and see me coming.

WELCOME HOME, SOLDIER

I got out of the cab, threw my duffle bag on my shoulder, rounded the street corner, and came in view of the house. I had just walked a few steps when out of the house and up the road came my wife. Following her came my sister, dad, and mom. I dropped my bag, caught my wife in my arms, kissed her, and then hugged my mother, dad, and sister. On the side of the house, they had hung a large sign saying, "Welcome Home!"

Yes, I was home at last.

Published by:

Bluewater Publications is a multi-faceted publishing company capable of meeting all of your reading and publishing needs. Our twofold aim is to:

1) Provide the market with educationally enlightening and inspiring research and reading materials
2) Make the opportunity of being published available to any author or researcher who desires to become published

We are passionate about preserving history; whether it is through the republishing of an out-of-print classic or by publishing the research of historians and genealogists, Bluewater Publications is the publisher you need.

To learn more about the person who wrote this book or for information about how you can be published through Bluewater Publications, please visit:

www.BluewaterPublications.com

Confidently Preserving Our Past,
Angela Broyles
Bluewater Publications.com
Formerly known as Heart of Dixie Publishing